GUIDE TO
Economic
Indicators

GUIDE TO
Economic
Indicators

NORMAN FRUMKIN

M. E. SHARPE, INC.
Armonk, New York
London, England

Available in the United Kingdom and Europe from M. E. Sharpe,
Publishers, 3 Henrietta Street, London WC2E 8LU.

Library of Congress Cataloging-in-Publication Data

Frumkin, Norman.
  Guide to economic indicators / by Norman Frumkin.
      p.   cm.
  Bibliography: p.
  ISBN 0-87332-521-4—ISBN 0-87332-620-2 (pbk.)
  1. Economic indicators—United States. 2. Business cycles—United
States—Statistics. 3. United States—Economic conditions—
Statistics. I. Title.
  HC103.F9   1989   88-35917
  330.973 '0021—dc19   CIP

Printed in the United States of America

                              ∞

BB   10   9   8   7   6   5   4   3

To Sarah, Jacob, and Samuel

CONTENTS

ILLUSTRATIONS

Figures

Tables

PREFACE

This book is a handy reference guide to indicators on the American economy for people who have no special background in economics. It is a practical tool for obtaining information quickly about the main characteristics of economic indicators which are frequently cited by economists, politicians, journalists, and others who comment on the current state of the economy.

The idea for the book came from Richard Bartel, editor of *Challenge*. I thank him for his advice and support. His encouragement was unfailing, as it was for *Tracking America's Economy*.

Many persons, including economists at the organizations that provide the indicators as well as analysts who use the indicators, reviewed particular sections of the book. Their comments were essential, and I appreciate their help and the time they took to give it. The book is much better for it. However, they gave advice only, and I am responsible for everything in the book. The reviewers were: William Alterman, Charles Anderson, Walt Arvin, Christopher Bach, Barry Beckman, Jason Bram, David Coe, John Coleman, Thomas Cuny, Richard Curtin, Jerry Donahoe, Eugene Epstein, Paul Flaim, Peter Frein, Sarah Frumkin, Seymour Gaylinn, Gary Gillum, Kenneth Goldstein, John Gorman, Gordon Green, David Hirschberg, Thomas Jabine, Patrick Jackman, Joanne Katz, Milton Kaufman, Zoltan Kenessey, Michael Leahy, Virginia Lewis, Charles Luckett, Elizabeth Lue de Grof, Jerome Mark, Paul Masson, William Mittendorf, Tiziana Mohorovic,

Geoffrey Moore, John Murphy, Albert Neubert, James O'Leary, Charles Ou, Bruce Phillips, Keith Phillips, Richard Pickering, Lois Plunkert, Richard Pombonyo, Eugene Seskin, Sandra Shaber, David Simon, Earl Stephens, Fred Thorp, Thomas Tibbetts, Theodore Torda, Joseph Wakefield, Patricia White, Donald Wood, Gaylord Worden, and Frederick Yohn.

Jody Foster was the style editor. She enhanced the overall presentation and language of the book with her unique perspective, insight, and literary talent. This was a major contribution, as was her editing of *Tracking America's Economy*.

Most important, while writing the book, I shared with my wife, Sarah, in the gifts of daily life.

INTRODUCTION

This book provides concise descriptions of over fifty economic indicators developed primarily by U.S. government agencies but also by private and international organizations. These indicators reflect the overall dimensions and international aspects of the American economy as well as particular segments of it.

This introduction briefly describes how these economic indicators are used to track the economy and provides some background material on using economic indicators, including how to interpret changes in them and how to evaluate their accuracy. The introduction concludes by explaining how the information in this book is arranged.

Interpreting Business Cycles with Economic Indicators

The economy continually operates in recurring phases of rising and falling activity which are referred to as business cycles. Economic indicators are used to measure overall economic activity to classify it as rising (expansion) or falling (recession), as well as to determine the cyclical turning points of these expansions and recessions. The actual and technical determination of expansions and recessions is made by a committee of economists under the auspices of the National Bureau of Economic Research (NBER), a private nonprofit economic research organization. The official designation of business cycles by this nongovernmental organization is accepted by a wide range of economists and politicians, regardless of their differing views regarding economic analysis and policy formulation.

The NBER committee does not rely on a specific formula. The committee bases its decision on judgments about the overall direction in which the preponderance of the indicators are moving. For example, in general, a recession is indicated when the real gross national product (GNP in constant dollars, which abstracts from rising or falling prices) declines for two successive quarters; however, such a decline doesn't necessarily result in the designation of a recession. Sometimes indicators move contrary to the overall trend. One of the challenges of economic analysis is to assess the import of such variations from the general trend.

Most analysis of economic indictors, then, is concerned with changes in the indicators over time—the cyclical fluctuations between expansion and growth and recession and decline. While the absolute volume or level of economic activity is of some interest, movements from one period to the next are more important for tracking the economy. The indicators often show change in terms of percent or as index numbers, making relative comparisons over long time periods easier. It is customary to think in terms of one year for assessing economic performance. Over the period of a year, of course, some changes simply reflect natural seasonal variations. Thus, to interpret indicators effectively, an analyst must understand index numbers, annualized and annual movements, and seasonality. In addition, because those indicators which are measured in dollars (such as the gross national product or wage earnings) are affected by increases and decreases in prices, the analyst must understand the measurement of indicators in constant dollars which abstract from these price changes.

Index Numbers

Economic data represent the myriad of transactions between buyers and sellers in consumer, industrial, labor, and financial markets involving both private parties and governments. In order to analyze this vast amount of detail, the transactions are summarized into groups and overall totals. One method of summarizing is through index numbers, which are a convenient way of quickly assessing the direction and level of changes in economic activity. Index numbers are typically associated with indicators of industrial production and prices, although they are also used for many other economic activities.

An index number starts with a base period, usually a single year or the average of a few consecutive years. The base period is defined as equivalent to 100, and all levels of activity of the indicator before and after the base period are represented as percentage differences from the base. For example, an index of 95 means that the indicator for that period (month, quarter, or year) is 5 percent below the base period, and an index of 128 means that the indicator is 28 percent above the base period. The formula for calculating the percent change between two periods is:

$$\frac{\text{Period 2}}{\text{Period 1}} - 1.0 \times 100$$

Thus, in the example,

$$\frac{128}{95} = 1.347 - 1.0 = 0.347 \times 100 = 34.7\%$$

Assuming 95 is the period 1 index and 128 is period 2 index, the percent change between the two periods is 34.7 percent.

The base period is typically selected according to the availability of detailed survey data. It also is desirable that the period be one during which the economy is relatively balanced, neither one that is booming with high inflation nor one that is depressed with high unemployment. However, this criterion is secondary. The availability of the required data dominates the determination of the base period.

There are two typical ways (but not the only ones) of using the base period as a point of departure in constructing the index. One is to assume that the relative importance of each item in the index (referred to as weights) is unchanged over time, and the only factor resulting in a change in the index is the movement of the components over time—for example, production for a production index or prices for a price index. The other is to assume that changes in the importance of one item to another in the index does occur, as one existing item is substituted for another or replaced by a new product because of changing prices and tastes and new technologies. In this case, changes in the index result from the effects of substitution and new products, as well as from the movement of the basic production or price characteristic of the index.

These differing methodologies affect the movements of production and price indexes over time. Both involve the quantity and price components of the value of each item in the index. For production indexes, when the relative price of each item is held constant from the base period, a higher rate of growth in production (or lower rate of production decline) typically appears over time compared to when the relative importance of each item reflects the current period price. This occurs because a new product with high growth rates often has a high price when introduced and the price subsequently declines as output expands. For price indexes, the effect of maintaining the same relative quantity of each item in the index over time tends to show a higher rate of price increase (or lower rate of price decline) than when each item in the index represents the actual items bought in each period as a result of buyers switching to lower-priced substitutes and new products (after the new product price declines).

Preference for using either methodology depends on the analytic use intended for the index. For example, when the focus is on measuring price change for purchasing the same items over time, a price index based on constant weights is used; but when the focus is on measuring price change for the actual items purchased, a current-weighted price index is used. It is sometimes difficult to determine which one more accurately reflects actual economic behavior. When two indexes are available for the same activity based on the alternative methodologies, changes over time may be considered as a range bounded by the lower and upper limits rather than as a single figure.

Annualized and Annual Movements

Three measures are related to annual trends: the seasonally adjusted annual rate, annual change, and December-to-December or fourth-quarter–to–fourth-quarter change.

The SEASONALLY ADJUSTED ANNUAL RATE (SAAR) reflects what the yearly movement of the indicator would be if the same rate of change (adjusted for seasonal variations) were to continue for the next eleven months (monthly indicator) or for the next three quarters (quarterly indicator). This figure represents the same rate of change for the current month or quarter compounded over the rest of the year. The SAAR provides a quick view of how a very short-term movement compares to a 12-month period. It also facilitates comparisons of growth rates for periods of differing lengths. However, it is important to recognize that SAAR figures assume a constant rate of change for comparative purposes only—they are not meant to forecast what is expected to occur.

ANNUAL CHANGE figures compare the average level of the indicator in one year to the average level of the next year. These averages are computed from data for the twelve months or four quarters of the indicator and, thus, help to compensate for the effects of unusually high or low activity periods when analyzing short periods during the year.

DECEMBER-TO-DECEMBER or FOURTH-QUARTER–TO–FOURTH-QUARTER CHANGE figures focus on economic change from the end of one calendar year to the end of the next calendar year. This kind of data is often used in economic reports at the beginning of the calendar year to predict the coming twelve months. It provides a more current assessment of the most recent and coming 12-month periods than the above annual change figures. However, any single period during the year may have abnormally high or low rates of economic growth or inflation. Because these data aren't averaged over an annual period, they can provide a distorted view of annual change.

Seasonality

There are many factors—such as changes in the weather, holidays, school vacations, yearly automobile model changes, annual tax returns, and so forth—which cause normal seasonal up and down movements in economic activity during the year. If not taken into account, these fluctuations could distort real trends in the economy. (See Figure 1, which charts retail sales during 1987 in both seasonally adjusted and unadjusted numbers.) For example, Christmas buying can make the economy look prosperous in December when, in fact, Christmas shopping is below average. Or the normal summer shutdown of auto assembly plants for the new model year can make the economy look dormant in the summer when, in fact, fewer plants have shut down than is typical. To prevent seasonal variations from distorting the economic picture, most economic data are seasonally adjusted.

Seasonal adjustment attempts to eliminate movements in economic indicators caused by such factors as increased sales in November and December due to Christmas shopping, decreased construction work in winter because of cold weather, and the large number of students looking for work in summer months. The adjustments are based on experience in previous years and capture typical movements which are expected from the average experience. Because they cannot indicate special circumstances in particular time periods, however, aberrations should be watched for in analyzing current trends.

For those indicators which are not seasonally adjusted, comparing trends of several consecutive months with the same months of the previous year is an indirect technique of seasonal adjustment which helps determine when the indicator is actually rising or falling. However, this method can't identify cyclical

Figure 1. **Seasonal Patterns of Retail Sales: 1987.**

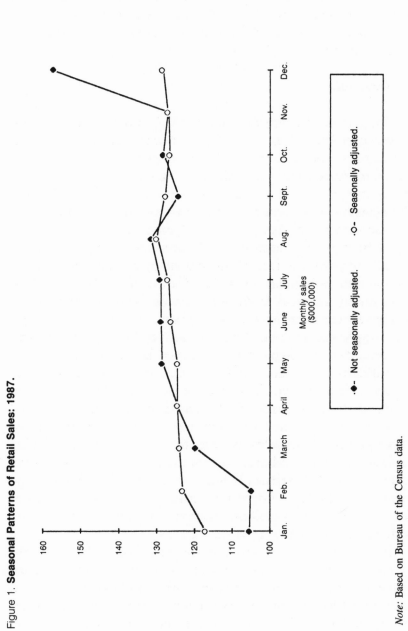

Note: Based on Bureau of the Census data.

turning points on a current basis because it focuses on year-to-year monthly change and doesn't provide a seasonally adjusted view of current movements in their own right.

It is beyond the scope of this book to detail the various statistical techniques of making seasonal adjustments or to analyze whether any particular indicator should be seasonally adjusted. However, the source publication of monthly or quarterly indicators and this book note whether, in fact, each indicator is seasonally adjusted or not.

Current Dollars vs. Constant Dollars

Many economic indicators are measured in current and constant dollars. Current dollars include the combined effect of changes in quantity and price over time and, thus, represent the DOLLAR VALUE of economic activity. For example, the value of retail sales of shoes includes the number of pairs of shoes multiplied by their unit prices. Constant dollars only include the effect of changes in quantity over time, which is the PHYSICAL VOLUME of economic activity. Constant dollar figures, which are stated in prices of a particular base period (such as 1977 dollars or 1982 dollars), are not affected by increases or decreases in prices. Because constant dollars are based on what the value would be if prices were the same as in the base period, they are a measure of quantity.

Constant dollar figures are difficult to relate to as actual figures because of price changes since the base period. For example, in 1989 it is difficult to think of average weekly earnings of workers in 1977 dollars. However, for some analyses, such as rates of economic growth or changes in workers' purchasing power, a measure of quantity (in constant dollars) rather than a measure of value (in current dollars) is the relevant figure. For example, it is far more meaningful to compare the change in weekly wages measured in constant dollars than in current dollars because of the effect of inflation on purchasing power. Thus, while wages in current dollars may have risen from one period to the next, wages in constant dollars may have declined because prices of goods and services that workers buy rose more than wages and, consequently, workers' purchasing power (or real income) declined.

Evaluating the Accuracy of Economic Indicators

There are many kinds of questions which can be raised about the accuracy of economic indicators. Conceptual issues, such as whether the indicators measure what they purport—for example, if the unemployment rate truly represents the proportion of people out of work or if the consumer price index truly represents inflation to the consumer—are beyond the scope of this book. More practical considerations, such as how closely the underlying data represent the definitions of the indicator, are also incapable of being measured. Such errors clearly do exist because secondary data are used as source information for constructing economic indicators. For example, data based on income tax returns which were originally developed for assessing the economic effects of existing income tax laws and of proposed changes in tax laws are used for estimating certain components of the gross national product and for obtaining information on small firms for the economic censuses. Even though some data sources may not exactly correspond to the definitional concepts of certain indicators, secondary sources are used in constructing economic indicators to hold down the costs of data collection and to limit the reporting burden on the public.

There are two fairly simple ways to evaluate the accuracy of economic indicators, however. The effect of data errors and the relative accuracy of an indicator can be estimated by taking into account the extent of revisions to the preliminary data and, in the case of indicators based on surveys, the sampling reliability of the surveys. Quantitative measures of the effect of these errors have been developed in some cases.

Error due to revision reflects changes in the figures from when

xxii   GUIDE TO ECONOMIC INDICATORS

they are initially provided to the later, more accurate information. The size of revision error is based on the past experience of these changes. For example, two-thirds of the revisions between the advance and latest estimates of real gross national product have been within a range of -1.9 to 2.8 percentage points. Thus, based on a 67 percent confidence, it is likely that an advance quarterly estimate of real GNP growth at an annual rate of 2.0 percent will be revised within a range of 0.1 to 4.8 percent. Raising the confidence level to 90 percent increases the likely revision from the advance figure of 2.0 percent to a range of -0.6 to 6.1 percent.

Error due to sampling results from the likelihood that data obtained from a sample of a population differ from what they would be if the entire population were surveyed. Estimates of sampling error are developed from mathematical formulas of probability, and there is a predetermined direct relationship between error size and its chances of occurring. For example, the sampling error for housing starts based on a 67 percent confidence is plus or minus 3 percent. Thus, at a confidence of 67 percent, it is likely that a monthly figure of housing starts at an annual rate of 1.5 million units ranges within 1.455 and 1.545 million if all starts were surveyed. Raising the confidence level to 95 percent doubles the sampling error for 1.5 million units to a range of 1.41 to 1.59 million.

When such estimates are available, it is important to take them into account. However, whether estimates of error are available or not, it is clear in all cases that any single number provided by an indicator cannot always exactly represent reality. Because of the various sources of error inherent in economic data, in general, an indicator should be considered as representing a range rather than an actual figure. Analysis of the specific or related data, as well as estimates of the size of revisions or sampling errors available, can suggest whether actual measurements fall closer to upper or lower bounds of that range.

Revisions

Economic indicators are developed from data gathered in surveys of households, businesses and governments, and from tax and regulatory reports submitted to federal and state governments. The indicators are available weekly, monthly, quarterly, or annually, depending on the data series. Because policymakers in the Administration, Congress, and Federal Reserve Board want the indicators as soon as possible following the month or quarter to which they refer, the figures are initially provided on a preliminary basis and are revised in subsequent months as more complete and accurate data are obtained. Revisions are sometimes substantial, and it is important that preliminary information be treated as tentative. The use of preliminary and revised information results from the tension between the needs for both timely and accurate data. In analyzing current information, it is desirable to view the most recent data in the context of previous trends and to wait for the more accurate revised data to determine if there has been a continuation or change from the trend.

Some sources provide a figure indicating the probable range of revisions. Typically, these are indicators developed from more than one data source, such as the gross national product and the industrial production index, or from surveys using nonprobability samples (see "Sampling Reliability" below).

In addition to revisions that are made on a current basis, more comprehensive revisions are made annually, every five years, or every ten years, depending on the indicator. These are referred to as "benchmark" revisions. For particular indicators, they result in a revision of all historical data, as in the case of the gross national product; in other cases, application of the new definitions and data-estimating methodologies is limited to future figures of the indicator, as for the consumer price index. The decision about whether to revise historical data is based on consideration of several factors—the need to have a consistent series over time balanced against the lack or weakness of comparable data for earlier time periods, the theoretical question of whether to "rewrite history" by including factors that previously weren't considered in economic analysis and policymaking, and the additional costs for statistical programs to make the more extensive revisions. When the historical data are not revised, there is a break in the series where the previous data are not fully consistent with the new data. These inconsistencies in data should be recognized when analyzing long-term trends.

The benchmark is more accurate because it is based on data obtained from a larger sample of survey respondents including, in some cases, the universe of the whole population, such as the five-year economic censuses and the ten-year census of population. It is also more accurate because there is more time to check the validity of the reported survey data. Thus, the benchmark provides more complete and precise information for checking the accuracy of the indicator at particular points in time and for revising historical data and estimating current data.

Sampling Reliability

A survey is typically based on a sample of respondents from the universe of the entire population being surveyed. Many indicators are based on a probability sample survey which represents all groups of the universe proportionate to the size of each group. However, it is unlikely that any single sample corresponds precisely to the distribution of groups in the universe. Thus, a sampling error is calculated to indicate the possible range of error in the survey data. The unemployment rate is an example of an economic indicator for which a sampling error is provided.

If a sample does not fully represent the components of the universe in accordance with the relative importance of each component, the survey isn't based on a probability sample. For indicators based on nonprobability samples, only revision error rates can be calculated. The survey of manufacturers' shipments, orders, and inventories is an example of an economic indicator for which a revision error, but not a sampling error, is provided.

However, even for probability samples, the present state of knowledge does not allow an estimate of the accuracy with which respondents answer survey questions. Error attributable to inaccurate answers is known as nonsampling or reporting error, and all survey data, including those obtained from the universe as well as from a sample, contain an unknown amount of such inaccuracy.

Using This Book

The more than 50 indicators described in this book are grouped under 40 generic categories. For example, several types of interest rates are grouped under the interest rate category. The book presents the indicators in alphabetic order so that readers may quickly locate a particular indicator. However, for analytical purposes, it is helpful to know how the indicators interrelate in describing the economy. Below, the indicators are grouped under common topics to help those with interest in a particular segment of the economy.

Topical Grouping of the Indicators

AGGREGATE DEMAND AND SUPPLY

Gross National Product
Personal Income and Saving
Consumer Confidence Index
 and Consumer Sentiment Index
Industrial Production Index
Capacity Utilization
Plant and Equipment Expenditures
Capital Appropriations
Manufacturers' Orders
Inventory-Sales Ratios
Housing Starts

LABOR

Unemployment
Employment
Help-wanted Advertising Index
Average Weekly Hours
Average Weekly Earnings
Productivity
Unit Labor Costs
Average Hourly Earnings Index
Employment Cost Index

INFLATION

Inflation
GNP Price Deflators and Indexes
Consumer Price Index
Producer Price Indexes
Import and Export Price Indexes
CRB Futures Price Index

FINANCE

Money Supply
Flow of Funds
Bank Loans: Commercial and Industrial
Consumer Installment Credit
Interest Rates
Stock Market Price Indexes and Dividend
  Yields

GOVERNMENT

Government Budgets and Debt

INTERNATIONAL

Balance of Trade: Merchandise Exports and Imports
Balance of Payments: International Economic Transactions
International Investment Position of the United States
Value of the Dollar

CYCLICAL INDICATORS

Leading, Coincident, and Lagging Indexes

ECONOMIC WELL-BEING

Distribution of Income
Poverty
Business Starts
Business Failures
Farm Parity Ratio

Format

The following format is used for the description of each indicator:

Introductory Statement. Capsule summary of what the indicator represents.

Where and When Available. Primary and secondary publication sources for obtaining the indicator and publication dates for the preliminary and revised information.

Content. Definition of the indicator and the scope of its coverage.

Methodology. Data and estimating techniques used in constructing the indicator.

Accuracy. Range of sampling or revision error in the indicator.

Relevance. Significance of the indicator for economic analysis and policymaking.

Recent Trends. Behavior of the indicator following the first oil price shock of the early 1970s to the late 1980s (1975–87).

Historical Data. Annual data for the indicator from 1975 through 1987 (based on statistics available in October 1988). The exception is the leading, coincident, and lagging indexes, which, because of a revision in methodology in 1989, incorporate the statistics available in March 1989.

References from Primary Data Source. Publications of the organization that provides the indicator which describes the first six items above.

To facilitate cross-referencing, indicators covered in the book are italicized whenever they are mentioned in sections other than those in which they are the primary focus.

Statistical Sources

Most of the indicators in this book are produced and published by federal government agencies. In the dissemination of economic statistics, there is a distinction between primary and secondary data. The term "primary data" refers to economic indicators published in magazines or reports by the organization that produces the figures, while "secondary data" refers to indicators published by organizations other than the producer of the figures. The following monthly magazines, which include both primary and secondary data, are the main vehicles for publishing the indicators: the *Survey of Current Business* and *Business Conditions Digest* of the Bureau of Economic Analysis in the U.S. Department of Commerce; the *Monthly Labor Review* of the Bureau of Labor Statistics in the U.S. Department of Labor; and the *Federal Reserve Bulletin* of the Federal Reserve Board. A handy secondary publication is the monthly *Economic Indicators*, which is prepared by the U.S. Council of Economic Advisers for the Joint Economic Committee of Congress. These publications are cited as primary or secondary sources of the indicators under the "Where and When Available" category. They are sold by the U.S. Government Printing Office. The appendix tables of the annual *Economic Report of the President* are the most convenient source for historical data; single copies are available free from the Executive Office of the President.

GUIDE TO
Economic
Indicators

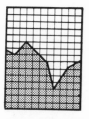

AVERAGE HOURLY EARNINGS INDEX

The average hourly earnings index represents changes in labor costs for money wages and salaries for production and nonsupervisory workers in private nonfarm industries. Fringe benefit costs are excluded. The index does not reflect the changing composition of employment between high and low wage industries, but it does reflect the changing composition of employment between high and low wage occupations within each industry. Thus, the index reflects labor costs associated with the actual changing types of jobs over time within industries, but does not reflect costs associated with the changing distribution of employment among industries.

(The average hourly earnings index was discontinued in 1989. It was replaced by an expansion of the *employment cost index* to include more specific industries and occupational groups. The earnings index is included here because it provides different kinds of information from the employment cost index: the earnings index includes historical data since the 1940s, while the employment cost index begins in 1976; the earnings index represents labor costs for the changing types of jobs over time, while the employment cost index focuses on labor costs for the same jobs over time; and the earnings index includes an estimate of costs in constant dollars, which the employment cost index lacks.)

Where and When Available

Data on the average hourly earnings index are provided monthly by the Bureau of Labor Statistics in the U.S. Department of Labor. The data are published in a press release and in two BLS monthly magazines, the *Monthly Labor Review* and *Employment and Earnings*. Secondary sources include *Economic Indicators*, the *Survey of Current Business*, and *Business Conditions Digest*.

The figures are available on the third Friday after the week containing the 12th of the month (which falls on the first or second Friday of the month) following the month to which they refer. On the day the monthly numbers are released, the Commissioner of Labor Statistics reports on recent employment and unemployment trends to the Joint Economic Committee of Congress. Preliminary data are provided for the immediately preceding month; these are revised in the subsequent two months. Annual revisions are made in June of the following year.

Content

The average hourly earnings index measures wages and salaries paid to production workers in manufacturing, as well as the wages, salaries, and commissions paid to nonsupervisory workers in other private nonagricultural industries. The index covers money wages including payments for paid vacations and sick leave. It excludes bonuses, tips, health, retirement, and other noncash fringe benefits, the employer's share of social security taxes, and in-kind payments such as free rent and food. Wage payments represent straight-time and premium rates (for example, the higher rates paid for work on holidays, at night, or under hazardous conditions). Earnings are excluded for office and sales workers in manufacturing and for supervisors and executives in all industries.

The indexes are provided in current dollars and in constant (1977) dollars. Because they reflect a fixed composition of employment in each industry, the indicators aren't affected by shifts in employment between higher and lower wage industries. However, they are affected by the changing composition of higher and lower paying occupations within each industry.

The average hourly earnings index is currently based on 1977 = 100.

The average hourly earnings figures are seasonally adjusted.

Methodology

The data for average hourly earnings are obtained from the survey of employer payrolls used to measure *employment*. The methodology of the survey is described in that section. Average hourly earnings are derived by dividing the payrolls by hours for all production or nonsupervisory employees in each industry. These industry averages are weighted by the relative importance of each industry's employment in 1977 to maintain a fixed composition of industry employment for the total index of all industries. The constant dollar figures are calculated by dividing actual earnings by the *consumer price index* for urban wage earners and clerical workers.

Accuracy

There are no estimates of sampling or revision error for the average hourly earnings index.

Relevance

The average hourly earnings index indicates underlying trends in industry wage costs. Since it doesn't take into account the changing composition of industry employment, the index works as a broad indicator of trends in industry wage rates as a component of business costs. The constant dollar index is an additional gauge of how trends in wage costs compare to other business costs.

However, it should be kept in mind that the average hourly earnings index excludes fringe benefits and includes the shifting composition of occupations within each industry. While changes in these items don't significantly affect short-term movements during the course of a year, they can become important over several years.

Recent Trends

The average hourly earnings index in current dollars increased at an accelerating rate during 1975–81 and, subsequently, at a decelerating rate during 1982–87. For example, after peaking at annual increases of 9 percent in 1980–81, the increases had slowed to 2.5 percent as of 1986–87.

In constant dollars, the index rose in 6 years and declined in 7 years over the 1975–87 period. Increases typically ranged from 1 to 1.5 percent. Decreases of 1 to 4 percent occurred in 1979–81, and decreases within 1 percent occurred in 1984, 1985, and 1987.

Table 1

Average Hourly Earnings Index

Index: 1977 = 100

	Current dollars	1977 dollars	Percent change from preceding year	
			Current dollars	1977 dollars
1975	86.7	97.6	8.4%	−0.7%
1976	92.9	99.0	7.2	1.4
1977	100.0	100.0	7.6	1.0
1978	108.2	100.5	8.2	0.5
1979	116.8	97.4	7.9	−3.1
1980	127.3	93.5	9.0	−4.0
1981	138.9	92.6	9.1	−1.0
1982	148.5	93.4	6.9	0.9
1983	155.4	94.9	4.6	1.6
1984	160.3	94.6	3.2	−0.3
1985	165.2	94.1	3.1	−0.5
1986	169.4	95.0	2.5	1.0
1987	173.5	94.0	2.5	−1.1

References from Primary Data Source

Bureau of Labor Statistics, U.S. Department of Labor, *BLS Handbook of Methods,* April 1988, Chapter 2.

C. Donald Wood, "Employment Cost Index series to replace Hourly Earnings Index," *Monthly Labor Review,* July 1988.

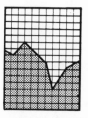

AVERAGE WEEKLY EARNINGS

Average weekly earnings represent the money income of workers in private nonagricultural industries. Because wages and salaries reflect the composition of employment in high-paying and low-paying industries and occupations, the figures are affected by changes in the composition of these employment characteristics.

Where and When Available

Data on average weekly earnings of workers are provided monthly by the Bureau of Labor Statistics in the U.S. Department of Labor. The data are published in a press release and in two monthly BLS magazines, the *Monthly Labor Review* and *Employment and Earnings*. Secondary sources include *Economic Indicators* and the *Survey of Current Business*.

The figures are available on the third Friday after the week containing the 12th of the month (which falls on the first or second Friday of the month) following the month to which they refer. On the day the monthly numbers are published, the Commissioner of Labor Statistics reports on recent employment and unemployment trends to the Joint Economic Committee of Congress. Preliminary data are provided for the immediately preceding month; these are revised in the subsequent two months. Annual revisions are made in June of the following year.

Content

Average weekly earnings data cover the wages and salaries of production workers in manufacturing industries, as well as the wages, salaries, and commissions of nonsupervisory workers in other private nonagricultural industries. Earnings include wages for time at work and for paid vacations, sick leave, holidays, and overtime (whether or not a premium is paid for overtime). Bonuses, tips, and in-kind payments such as free rent and meals are excluded, as are health, retirement, and other noncash fringe benefits, as well as the employer share of social security taxes. Earnings are excluded for office and sales workers in manufacturing and for supervisors and executives in all industries.

The data are provided in current dollars and in constant (1977) dollars.

The average weekly earnings figures are seasonally adjusted.

Methodology

The data for weekly earnings are obtained from the survey of employer payrolls used to measure *employment*. The methodology of the survey is described in that section. There is no independent benchmark figure for weekly earnings; the figures are revised every June with the annual employment benchmark to reflect revisions in the distribution of employment among industries. Average weekly earnings are derived by multiplying *average weekly hours* by average hourly earnings. The constant dollar figures are calculated by dividing actual earnings by the *consumer price index* for urban wage earners and clerical workers.

Accuracy

There are no estimates of sampling or revision error for average weekly earnings.

Relevance

Average weekly earnings data are based on job-related earnings of workers of modest income. Currently, this working population of civilian family households and unrelated individuals accounts for approximately one-third of the noninstitutional population (people outside of jails, old age homes, long-term medical care, and other sheltered housing). The earnings figures are relevant for several reasons. First, they provide a measure of consumer purchasing power as indicated by changes in wage earnings for an important segment of the spending public. Second, because they gauge the economic well-being of workers, their trends may track the direction of future wage demands. Finally, comparisons of wages in different industries help to indicate the types of jobs being created.

Table 2

Average Weekly Earnings

	Current dollars	1977 dollars	Percent change from preceding year	
			Current dollars	1977 dollars
1975	$163.53	$184.16	5.7%	−3.1%
1976	175.45	186.85	7.3	1.5
1977	189.00	189.00	7.7	1.2
1978	203.70	189.31	7.8	0.2
1979	219.91	183.41	8.0	−3.1
1980	235.10	172.74	6.9	−5.8
1981	255.20	170.13	8.5	−1.5
1982	267.26	168.09	4.7	−1.2
1983	280.70	171.26	5.0	1.9
1984	292.86	172.78	4.3	0.9
1985	299.09	170.42	2.1	−1.4
1986	304.85	171.07	1.9	0.4
1987	312.50	169.28	2.5	−1.0

Recent Trends

From the late 1970s to the late 1980s, average weekly earnings in constant dollars declined, in general. Declines in real earnings occurred in 7 of the 13 years over the 1975–87 period. After rising 2.8 percent from 1975 to 1978, real earnings declined 10.6 percent between 1978–87.

Reference from Primary Data Source

Bureau of Labor Statistics, U.S. Department of Labor, *BLS Handbook of Methods,* April 1988, Chapter 2.

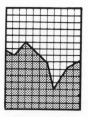

AVERAGE WEEKLY HOURS

Average weekly hours represent the length of the workweek in private nonagricultural industries. The figures are affected by changes in both the industrial and occupational composition of employment.

Where and When Available

Data on average weekly hours in the workplace are provided monthly by the Bureau of Labor Statistics in the U.S. Department of Labor. The data are published in a press release and two monthly BLS magazines, the *Monthly Labor Review* and *Employment and Earnings*. Secondary sources include *Economic Indicators*, the *Survey of Current Business*, and *Business Conditions Digest*.

The figures are available on the third Friday after the week containing the 12th of the month (which falls on the first or second Friday of the month) following the month to which they refer. On the day the monthly numbers are released, the Commissioner of Labor Statistics reports on recent employment and unemployment trends to the Joint Economic Committee of Congress. Preliminary data are provided for the immediately preceding month; these are revised in the subsequent two months. Annual revisions are made in June of the following year.

Content

Average weekly hours measure weekly time on the job, including straight-time and overtime hours (whether or not a premium is paid for overtime), for the average of full-time and part-time workers. The inclusion of paid absences from work means that hours are counted on the basis of "hours paid for" rather than "hours worked." The hours information includes production workers in manufacturing industries and nonsupervisory workers in other industries. Hours are excluded for office and sales workers in manufacturing and for executives in all industries.

Separate data on overtime hours are provided for manufacturing industries. These are defined to include worktime for which premium pay is received beyond the straight-time workday or workweek. Holiday hours are included only if premium wages are paid. Hours associated with incentive pay for shift differentials such as night or weekend work, hazardous conditions, or similar situations are excluded. Because these separate data on overtime are limited to work for premium pay, they differ from the overtime included in average weekly hours which includes *all* overtime even if no premium pay is involved.

The average weekly hours figures are seasonally adjusted.

Methodology

The data for hours are obtained from the survey of employer payrolls used to measure *employment*. The methodology of the survey is described in that section. There is no independent benchmark figure for weekly hours; they are revised every June with the annual employment benchmark because of revisions in the composition of employment among industries. Weekly hours are derived by dividing total hours paid for by the number of employees during the pay period. These are adjusted for pay periods that are longer than one week so that they represent a seven-day period. Separate data are collected on the survey form for overtime hours.

Accuracy

Although the hours data aren't based on a probability sample, an estimate of errors due to sampling has been developed assuming a random sample. This indicates that the relative error is plus or minus 0.1 percent.

Relevance

Average weekly hours are a sensitive barometer of labor demand. Employers generally prefer to increase or decrease hours worked before hiring or laying off workers in response to changes in *manufacturers' orders*, *inventory-sales ratios*, or planned production schedules. This is particularly true when the changes in the demand for labor are small or are expected to be temporary. Weekly hours in manufacturing is a component of the leading index of *leading, coincident, and lagging indexes*. The monthly

Table 3

Average Weekly Hours

	All private nonagricultural industries	Manufacturing industries	Overtime in manufacturing industries
1975	36.1	39.5	2.6
1976	36.1	40.1	3.1
1977	36.0	40.3	3.5
1978	35.8	40.4	3.6
1979	35.7	40.2	3.3
1980	35.3	39.7	2.8
1981	35.2	39.8	2.8
1982	34.8	38.9	2.3
1983	35.0	40.1	3.0
1984	35.2	40.7	3.4
1985	34.9	40.5	3.3
1986	34.8	40.7	3.4
1987	34.8	41.0	3.7

volatility of weekly hours makes discerning a short-term trend difficult. Movements over several months should be assessed when analyzing trends.

Recent Trends

The average weekly hours worked in all private nonagricultural industries decreased by 1 hour from 36 hours in the late 1970s to 35 hours in the late 1980s. Overall, weekly hours in manufacturing industries rose by close to 1 hour from the late 1970s to the late 1980s, reaching 41 hours in 1987. However, during 1978–82 manufacturing hours declined 1.5 hours. Overtime in manufacturing generally fluctuated within a range of 3.0 to 3.5 hours, although they fell to 2.6 hours in 1975 and rose to 3.7 hours in 1987.

Reference from Primary Data Source

Bureau of Labor Statistics, U.S. Department of Labor, *BLS Handbook of Methods,* April 1988, Chapter 2.

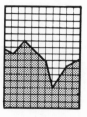

BALANCE OF PAYMENTS: INTERNATIONAL ECONOMIC TRANSACTIONS

The balance of payments accounts are the most comprehensive measure of U.S. international economic transactions with other countries. The transactions include exports and imports of goods and services, transfer payments such as pensions and government grants, and changes in U.S. and foreign holdings of financial assets and liabilities associated with international monetary reserves, loans, investments, and securities transactions. The various "balances" focus on the difference between exports and imports and international flows of transfer payments, but exclude financial assets and liabilities. When exports exceed imports, the balance is in surplus, and when imports exceed exports, the balance is in deficit. A surplus balance is generally referred to as "favorable" and a deficit as "unfavorable."

Where and When Available

The Bureau of Economic Analysis in the U.S. Department of Commerce provides quarterly measures of the balance of payments. They are published in a press release and in BEA's monthly magazine, the *Survey of Current Business*. Secondary sources include *Economic Indicators*, the *Federal Reserve Bulletin*, and *Business Conditions Digest*.

The figures are available 75 days after the quarter to which they refer. They are initially revised in the succeeding quarter and

15

then subsequently in June of the following year as part of the annual revisions. The annual revisions also change the figures for several of the preceding years. Constant dollar measures are published as part of the *gross national product*.

Content

Conceptually, the balance of payments is composed of two broad components. One is foreign trade in goods and services plus unilateral transfers. The other is the money and capital flows necessary to finance trade, transfers, and grants. The two components are definitionally equivalent but don't match statistically because of inadequacies in the data. The difference caused by these data problems is noted as the "statistical discrepancy."

Balance of payments data are provided for total U.S. transactions with all nations and separate transactions with particular nations and regions of the world. The United States includes the 50 states and the District of Columbia, Puerto Rico (except transactions between the states and Puerto Rico), and the Virgin Islands.

The balance of payments figures are in current dollars. They are converted to constant dollars for the *gross national product*.

Several elements comprise the foreign trade, transfer, and grant categories of the balance of payments. EXPORTS AND IMPORTS OF GOODS AND SERVICES encompass merchandise trade in the *balance of trade* plus the following: transfers under the foreign military sales program; defense purchases; passenger and freight transportation between the United States and other countries provided by American and foreign companies; other services provided by Americans and foreigners, such as insurance, telecommunications, construction, and engineering; income from royalties and license fees; and dividend and interest income paid by Americans and foreigners on foreign investments.

UNILATERAL TRANSFERS are nonmilitary government grants for which no payment is expected, such as foreign aid shipments of food, private and government pension payments by the U.S. government to American workers living in foreign countries and by other nations to foreign workers living in the United States, and gifts sent abroad by individuals and nonprofit organizations.

MILITARY GRANTS are items supplied by the U.S. government to foreign countries which exclude repayment.

Increases or decreases in U.S. assets abroad and foreign assets in the United States measure the means of financing the above foreign trade in goods and services, unilateral transfers, and military grants. The main elements of U.S. ASSETS ABROAD are as follows. U.S. GOVERNMENT OFFICIAL RESERVE ASSETS include the U.S. gold stock, special drawing rights and reserve position in the International Monetary Fund, and U.S. Treasury and Federal Reserve holdings of foreign currencies. OTHER GOVERNMENT ASSETS include loans to foreign nations and to U.S. private parties for investment abroad, capital contributions to international organizations except the IMF, and U.S. holdings of foreign currencies and other short-term assets associated with foreign aid programs and financial operations such as guarantee programs of the Export-Import Bank. U.S. PRIVATE ASSETS include direct investment abroad (ownership of at least 10 percent of foreign companies) by U.S. private parties, U.S. private holdings of foreign bonds and stocks, and U.S. bank and nonbank loans to foreigners.

The main elements of FOREIGN ASSETS IN THE UNITED STATES are as follows. FOREIGN OFFICIAL ASSETS are investments by foreign governments in U.S. government securities, U.S. government liabilities for foreign deposits in advance of delivery of foreign military sales items, and foreign government holdings of U.S. corporate debt and equity securities and of state and local government securities. OTHER FOREIGN ASSETS are direct investment in the United States (ownership of at least 10 percent of American companies) by foreign private parties; private foreign holdings of U.S. Treasury securities, state and local government securities, as well as corporate debt and equity securities; and loans to Americans by foreign banks and nonbanks.

The indicator provides four separate balances of exports minus imports: (1) merchandise trade; (2) goods and services; (3) goods, services, and remittances (remittances are government and private unilateral transfers excluding government grants); and (4) balance on current account (goods, services, and all unilateral transfers). Balances aren't calculated for changes in financial assets and liabilities because meaningful distinctions are difficult to make for such categories as short-term and long-term capital.

The balance of payments figures are seasonally adjusted.

Methodology

Information for the balance of payments figures comes from several sources. Data for merchandise exports and imports are based mainly on Census Bureau surveys (see *balance of trade*). The main sources for the other components are: BEA surveys of incoming and outgoing foreign direct investment; BEA surveys of average international traveler expenditures and U.S. Immigration and Naturalization Service data on the number of travelers; BEA surveys of international operations of U.S. and foreign ship operators and airlines; Treasury Department surveys (conducted by the Federal Reserve Bank of New York) of international assets and liabilities of U.S. banks and nonbank companies; and reports by the Department of Defense on foreign military sales and the Department of Agriculture on foreign aid shipments of food.

The quarterly figures are based on reported data for most items and estimates for those for which reported data are available either annually or less frequently. They are revised every June when more complete information is available. These revisions change some of the components for the past three to five years.

The constant dollar figures are derived by deflating the current dollar figures by the *import and export price indexes*, the defense and gross domestic product implicit price deflators from the *gross national product*, and foreign consumer price indexes (adjusted for changes in the *value of the dollar*).

The statistical discrepancy is defined as the accounting difference between the sum of credits and debits in the balance of payments. Credits are exports of goods and services, unilateral transfers to the United States, capital inflows or a decrease in

U.S. assets, decrease in U.S. official assets, and increase in foreign official assets in the United States. Debits are imports of goods and services, unilateral transfers to foreigners, capital outflows or increase in U.S. assets, increase in U.S. official reserve assets, and decrease in foreign official assets in the United States. A discrepancy results from the fact that data for the various components are developed independently and, consequently, aren't fully consistent in coverage, definition, timing, and accuracy. The discrepancy is a net figure in which overstatement of one data element is offset by understatement of another data element. When the discrepancy is positive, it signifies unrecorded funds entering the United States; a negative discrepancy indicates unrecorded funds leaving the United States.

Accuracy

There are no estimates of sampling or revision error in the balance of payments figures. Since offsetting errors among the data elements may reduce the statistical discrepancy, that figure provides an overall minimum magnitude of the net inconsistencies in the various data sources.

Relevance

The balance of payments reflects U.S. participation in world markets overall. It points up the relative importance of international product markets to our economy and indicates those markets which are gaining or losing ground. It also highlights shifts in international investment, including the effect on interest flows and dividend flows entering and leaving the United States. The extent to which the United States consumes and produces for world markets affects the *gross national product*.

The impact of international transactions, including their financing, affects the *value of the dollar* and American competitiveness. When Americans spend and invest more money abroad than foreigners spend and invest in the United States, the value of

Table 4

Balance of Payments: International Economic Transactions
(billions of dollars)

	Exports of goods and services (includes receipts of invest- ment income)	Imports of goods and services (includes payments of invest- ment income)	Unilateral transfers (excess of flows abroad over flows to U.S. = minus)	U.S. assets abroad (increase in capital outflow = minus)	Foreign assets in the U.S. (increase in capital inflow = plus)
1975	155.7	132.7	−4.9	−39.7	15.7
1976	171.6	−162.1	−5.3	−51.3	36.5
1977	184.3	−193.8	−5.0	−34.8	51.3
1978	220.0	−229.9	−5.6	−61.1	64.0
1979	286.8	−281.7	−6.1	−64.3	38.8
1980	342.5	−333.0	−7.6	−86.1	58.1
1981	376.5	−362.2	−7.5	−111.0	83.0
1982	349.6	−349.3	−9.0	−121.2	93.7
1983	334.5	−371.3	−9.5	−49.8	84.9
1984	360.8	−455.7	−12.1	−22.3	102.6
1985	360.6	−460.7	−15.1	−32.6	129.9
1986	375.1	−498.6	−15.3	−98.0	221.3
1987	424.8	−565.3	−13.4	−76.0	211.5

	Statistical discrepancy	Balance on merchandise trade	Balance on goods and services
1975	5.9	8.9	23.0
1976	10.5	−9.5	9.5
1977	−2.0	−31.1	−9.5
1978	12.5	−33.9	−9.9
1979	25.4	−27.5	5.1
1980	25.0	−25.5	9.5
1981	19.9	−28.0	14.3
1982	36.1	−36.4	0.3
1983	11.2	−67.1	−36.8
1984	26.8	−112.5	−95.0
1985	17.8	−122.1	−100.1
1986	15.6	−144.5	−123.5
1987	18.5	−160.3	−140.5

the dollar tends to decrease; greater spending and investment by foreigners in the United States tends to raise the dollar.

A large balance of payments deficit limits the flexibility of the Federal Reserve Board in conducting monetary policy (see *balance of trade*). Large deficits also create a growing foreign debt which raises interest payments to foreigners and thereby reduces the standard of living for Americans.

Recent Trends

Trade in goods and services changed significantly during 1975–87. From the late 1970s through 1982, both exports and imports were in close balance, with most years showing a small surplus. From 1983 to 1987, imports rose much faster than exports, resulting in a growing deficit reaching $141 billion in 1987.

Trends in U.S. assets abroad and foreign assets in the United States also differed between the early and later segments of the period. From 1975 to 1982, U.S. asset outflows exceeded foreign asset inflows except in 1977 and 1978, with the differential rising to $30 billion in the early 1980s. A reversal began in 1983 when foreign inflows were substantially and increasingly larger than U.S. outflows, with the differential reaching $135 billion in 1987.

The statistical discrepancy generally grew during the late 1970s and early 1980s, reaching $36 billion in 1982. It subsequently declined and then stabilized at around $16–19 billion during 1985–87. The plus sign during the entire 1975–87 period (except 1977) indicates that, on a net basis, the statistical reporting system persistently underestimated funds entering the United States.

Reference from Primary Data Source

Christopher L. Bach, "U.S. International Transactions, First Quarter 1978," Explanatory Notes, *Survey of Current Business,* Part II, June 1978.

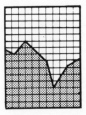

BALANCE OF TRADE:
MERCHANDISE EXPORTS
AND IMPORTS

The balance of trade represents foreign trade in merchandise (merchandise is goods as distinct from services). The "balance" represents the difference between exports and imports. When exports exceed imports, the balance is in surplus, and when imports exceed exports, the balance is in deficit. A surplus is usually referred to as a favorable balance and a deficit as an unfavorable balance. (International transactions in services and investments are included in the *balance of payments*.)

Where and When Available

Two agencies provide balance of trade figures. The Bureau of the Census in the U.S. Department of Commerce provides monthly figures, and the Bureau of Economic Analysis in the U.S. Department of Commerce provides monthly and quarterly figures. The data from the two agencies are based on different definitions. The Census measures are published in a press release, in *Highlights of U.S. Export and Import Trade*, and in the more detailed reports *FT 135: U.S. General Imports and Imports for Consumption* and *FT 410: U.S. Exports*. Secondary sources include *Economic Indicators*, the *Survey of Current Business*, *Federal Reserve Bulletin*, and *Business Conditions Digest*. The BEA monthly figures are provided on an unpublished basis to subscribers, and the quarterly figures are published in a press release and in BEA's monthly magazine, the *Survey of Current Business*. Constant dollar figures are published as part of the *gross national product*. Secondary sources include *Economic Indicators*, the *Federal Reserve Bulletin*, and *Business Conditions Digest*.

The Census figures are available 45 days after the month to which they refer. They are initially revised the following month and subsequently in quarterly and annual reports. The BEA monthly figures are available 55 days after the month to which they refer, and the quarterly figures are available 75 days after the quarter to which they refer. They are initially revised in the succeeding month and quarter and subsequently in June of the following year as part of the annual *balance of payments* revisions.

Content

Merchandise export and import data are provided for U.S. total foreign trade with all nations, plus detail for trade with particular nations and regions of the world as well as for individual commodities. U.S. trade includes that of the 50 states and the District of Columbia, Puerto Rico, and the Virgin Islands. The trade figures exclude shipments between the United States and the Commonwealth of Puerto Rico, the Virgin Islands, and other American possessions; however, supplementary figures are provided on U.S. export and import trade with Puerto Rico, U.S. exports to the Virgin Islands, and imports from Guam, American Somoa, and the Northern Mariana Islands.

The monthly Census and the BEA monthly and quarterly figures are in current dollars. In addition, the quarterly BEA figures are converted to constant dollars for the *gross national product*. The monthly Census figures will be provided in constant dollars beginning in 1990.

Exports cover domestically produced goods plus imported items that subsequently are exported without substantial physical change to the imported item (referred to as a re-export). Exports are valued at the dollar price at the U.S. port of export. This includes inland transportation, insurance, and other costs to deliver the merchandise alongside the ship or plane, but it excludes overseas transportation, insurance, and other charges beyond the U.S. port (referred to as f.a.s., free alongside ship). The month of exportation is the month that the shipment leaves the United States.

Imports cover goods for immediate consumption plus those stored in Customs bonded warehouses and in U.S. Foreign Trade Zones. They are valued in two ways. One is the Customs value, which is essentially equivalent to the f.a.s. price at the foreign port of export (see exports above). The other is the Customs/f.a.s. value plus overseas transportation, insurance, and other charges in delivering the merchandise to the United States (referred to as c.i.f., cost-insurance-freight). Both measures exclude U.S. import duties. The month of importation is the month when the Customs Bureau releases the merchandise to the importer. Census presents separate figures using both the f.a.s. and the c.i.f. valuations and BEA only uses the Customs/f.a.s. valuation.

The main distinction between the Census and BEA figures is that BEA adjusts the Census measures to conform to the *balance of payments* concepts. This results in three primary differences: (1) foreign military sales identified in Census documents are excluded by BEA but included elsewhere in the balance of payments accounts; (2) electric energy imports from Canada (until 1989) and inland truck and rail freight costs to the Canadian border for exports to and imports from Canada are excluded by Census and included by BEA (beginning in 1989 electric energy imports from Canada are included in the Census figures); and (3) the Census figures only include nonmonetary gold that is shipped across international borders, while BEA figures also include nonmonetary gold that changes ownership through book entries without being shipped across international borders. Nonmonetary gold represents all trade in gold in which at least one of the parties to the transaction is a private party; it excludes gold movements between governments, central banks, and international monetary institutions. Monetary gold represents gold movements between the U.S. Treasury or the Federal Reserve

Board acting for the Treasury and foreign governments or their central banks and the International Monetary Fund.

The balance of trade figures are seasonally adjusted.

Methodology

The basic data on merchandise exports and imports are developed from surveys conducted by the Census Bureau. They are adjusted by the BEA to reflect the balance of payments measures.

Bureau of the Census. The export statistics are derived mainly from mandatory information supplied by commercial exporters to the Customs Bureau, which provides the data to the Census Bureau. Customs checks the accuracy of those exports requiring licenses from the State Department for military items and from the Commerce Department for nonmilitary strategic materials. These figures are supplemented by data from some exporters who report their shipments directly to Census. In addition, the Department of Defense reports military aid shipments data to Census. Export data for shipments over $1,500 are compiled from the universe (100 percent sample) of all such reports. These account for 98 percent of all exports. Shipments under $1,501 are estimated from factors based on ratios of low-valued exports to total exports in past periods. (The threshold dollar exemption for low-valued exports from reporting requirements is raised from time to time, most recently in January 1987.)

The import statistics are derived from mandatory information supplied by importers to the Customs Bureau, which reviews the documents for accuracy and provides the corrected data to Census. Import data for shipments over $1,000 are compiled from the universe (100 percent sample) of all such reports. These account for 96 percent of all imports. Shipments under $1,001 are estimated from factors based on ratios of low-valued imports to total imports for past periods. (The threshold dollar exemption, exempting low-valued imports from reporting requirements, is raised from time to time, most recently in January 1985.)

Bureau of Economic Analysis. The statistical adjustments made to conform the Census data to the balance of payments measures are based on separate information obtained from a variety of sources, such as the Department of Defense for military exports, a BEA estimate for inland freight costs for Canadian foreign trade, the Department of Energy for imports of electric energy from Canada, and the Federal Reserve Board for nonmonetary gold trade.

The constant dollar measures are derived mainly by deflating the current dollar figures by the *import and export price indexes.* These are supplemented for a small number of items by the Census Bureau unit value indexes, which are imprecise price measures of foreign traded goods.

Accuracy

There are no estimates of sampling or revision error in the balance of trade figures. Since practically all of the Census data are based on surveys of the universe of exporters and importers, any sampling error for low-valued shipments would be insignificant. The monthly trade statistics are notoriously volatile from month to month.

Relevance

The balance of trade impacts the *gross national product, employment, inflation,* and the *value of the dollar.* It also has long-term implications for U.S. independence in managing our economy and for our standard of living. Export and import levels are influenced by economic growth at home and abroad and by the competitive position of American products in international markets and foreign goods in U.S. markets.

A surplus in the trade balance or a reduction in the trade deficit stimulates economic growth and job expansion, while a deficit or reduction in the surplus restrains economic growth and employment. This occurs because exports are produced in the United States and thus generate American production and employment, while American spending for imports stimulates production and employment abroad.

Over the long run, imports tend to hold down inflation because imports compete with American goods. Imports also moderate inflation during temporary shortages of domestic goods by providing a supplementary supply. Shortages may occur when drought or frost reduces food harvests; when an unexpected surge occurs in consumption; or when sudden bottlenecks appear in the production of lumber, paper, or other products for which domestic supply can't be expanded readily.

A large balance of trade deficit limits the flexibility of the Federal Reserve Board in conducting monetary policy for managing the economy. The deficit is financed by borrowing from domestic lenders or from abroad. Borrowing from domestic lenders to finance the deficit could lead to higher *interest rates*, unless accommodated by an increase in the *money supply*, which in turn may raise the rate of *inflation*. Borrowing from abroad can lead to a rise in the *value of the dollar*: the influx of foreign funds into the United States bids up the dollar compared to other currencies, which worsens the deficit by making exports more expensive and imports cheaper.

A continuing large deficit financed from abroad creates a growing foreign debt. Over the long run, this results in greater amounts of money paid in interest as payments to foreigners. Thus, U.S. incomes are reduced, as well as the standard of living.

Recent Trends

The deficit in the merchandise trade balance increased sharply from 1975 to 1987. Following a noticeable jump in 1977 from the relatively low deficits or surpluses of previous years, the deficit hovered around $30 billion annually from the late 1970s through the early 1980s. The deficit then rose substantially from 1983 to 1987, ranging in 1987 from $152–170 billion, depending on the definition.

Generally, the deficit under the Census import f.a.s. definition is lowest and that for the Census import c.i.f. is highest, with the BEA balance of payments deficit measure somewhere between the two. In 1987, the deficits were: Census f.a.s., −$152 billion;

BEA balance of payments, −$160 billion; and Census c.i.f., −$170 billion.

Table 5

Balance of Trade: Merchandise Exports and Imports (billions of dollars)

	Census trade, f.a.s.			BEA balance of payments, f.a.s.		
	Exports	Imports (f.a.s.)	Balance	Exports	Imports (f.a.s.)	Balance
1975	108.9	98.5	10.4	107.1	98.2	8.9
1976	116.8	123.5	−6.7	114.7	124.2	−9.5
1977	123.2	150.4	−27.2	120.8	151.9	−31.1
1978	145.8	174.8	−28.9	142.1	176.0	−33.9
1979	186.4	209.5	−23.1	184.5	212.0	−27.5
1980	225.6	244.9	−19.3	224.3	249.8	−25.5
1981	238.7	261.0	−22.3	237.1	265.1	−28.0
1982	216.4	244.0	−27.5	211.2	247.6	−36.4
1983	205.6	258.0	−52.4	201.8	268.9	−67.1
1984	224.0	325.7	−101.7	219.9	332.4	−112.5
1985	218.8	345.3	−126.5	215.9	338.1	−122.1
1986	227.2	365.4	−138.3	224.0	368.5	−144.5
1987	254.1	406.2	−152.1	249.6	409.9	−160.3

	Census trade, c.i.f.		
	Exports	Imports (c.i.f.)	Balance
1980	225.6	257.0	−31.4
1981	238.7	273.4	−34.6
1982	216.4	254.9	−38.4
1983	205.6	269.9	−64.2
1984	224.0	346.4	−122.4
1985	218.8	352.5	−133.6
1986	227.2	382.3	−155.1
1987	254.1	424.4	−170.3

References from Primary Data Sources

Bureau of the Census, U.S. Department of Commerce, *Highlights of U.S. Export and Import Trade,* monthly.

Christopher L. Bach, "U.S. International Transactions, First Quarter 1978," Explanatory Notes, *Survey of Current Business,* Part II, June 1978.

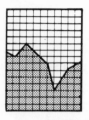

BANK LOANS:
COMMERCIAL AND INDUSTRIAL

Commercial and industrial bank loans are loans made by commercial banks to individuals, partnerships, and corporations for nonfarm business use. They also include bank loans made to investors for financial acquisitions such as company takeovers. The indicator thus focuses on loans made to income generating business activity as distinct from household consumer use.

Where and When Available

Commercial and industrial bank loan data are provided weekly and monthly by the Federal Reserve Board. They are published in three statistical releases and in the *Federal Reserve Bulletin*, the FRB's monthly magazine. Secondary sources include *Economic Indicators*, the *Survey of Current Business*, and *Business Conditions Digest*.

The weekly figures are available every Friday for the week ending Wednesday of the previous week. The monthly figures are available the fourth week of the month after the month to which they refer. The measures are revised on a continuing basis with the receipt of more accurate data.

Content

Commercial and industrial bank loans represent loans outstanding. Therefore, they include existing loans from the previous period and new loans, minus those repaid during the period. Secured and unsecured loans are included. In addition to traditional loans extended to borrowers, the data include nonfinancial commercial paper (negotiable notes sold by nonfinancial businesses) and bankers acceptances (bills which banks pledge their credit for on behalf of their customers). Bank loans, excluding commercial paper and bankers acceptances, are provided separately for borrowers whose primary address is the United States (including Puerto Rico and U.S. territories) from those with foreign addresses.

The data exclude loans to farmers, securities and real estate firms, other banks, companies that mainly extend business or personal credit, commercial paper of financial institutions bought by banks, and loans secured by real estate. No figures are available on the distribution of short-term and long-term loans.

Methodology

The bank loan data are obtained from weekly reports of a sample of Federal Reserve member and nonmember banks, both large and small, and from quarterly reports for banks not reporting weekly. Data on commercial paper and bankers acceptances are based on weekly reports of large banks. The weekly and monthly figures for all commercial banks include estimates for banks not reporting weekly. Estimates for the nonweekly reporting banks are based on relationships developed from the quarterly reports of all banks, those reporting weekly and those reporting quarterly. The bank loan figures are benchmarked to the quarterly reports twice a year.

Accuracy

Estimates of revisions to the bank loan figures are encompassed within a larger statistical category of "bank credit," which includes commercial and industrial and other bank loans plus U.S. government and other securities owned by banks. Revisions for this much broader category are within plus or minus a 0.5 percentage point of the annual growth rate of bank credit. The commercial and industrial bank loan component probably has a larger revision error, although the actual range is not known.

Relevance

The bank loan data provide a clue to business' willingness to go into debt. For analytical purposes, the monthly change and the monthly level are viewed differently. A rapid increase in bank loans suggests an optimistic outlook for business prospects, while a slow rate of loan expansion indicates a cautious business outlook.

By contrast, the simple existence of debt is a burden to business because of the principal and interest payments. Thus, existing

Table 6

Bank Loans: Commercial and Industrial

	Loans outstanding (billions of dollars) December	Annual percent change Dec. to Dec.	Annual percent change adjusted* Dec. to Dec.
1975	$189.3	−3.7%	−3.8%
1976	190.9	0.8	1.5
1977	211.0	10.5	10.5
1978	246.2	16.7	15.8
1979	291.4	18.4	17.0
1980	325.7	11.8	11.5
1981	355.4	9.1	12.5
1982	392.6	10.5	11.9
1983	414.1	5.5	5.6
1984	472.8	14.2	14.9
1985	499.4	5.6	5.5
1986	535.6	7.2	7.2
1987	565.5	5.6	5.6

*Adjusted for definitional changes in the loan data.

debt becomes a depressant to further borrowing. The monthly level of existing commercial and industrial loans (in constant dollars) is a component of the lagging index of the *leading, coincident, and lagging indexes*.

Recent Trends

After the rapid growth of bank loans in the late 1970s, loans increased at a much slower rate in the 1980s. For example, annual percentage increases during 1985–87 were one-half to one-third the increases during 1977–80. The earlier period was characterized by relatively higher interest rates and inflation. While higher interest rates would normally lead to a slowdown in loan demand, this didn't happen in the late 1970s. Apparently, the expectation of still higher interest rates during the earlier inflationary period overrode the historical tendency for higher interest rates to suppress borrowing.

Reference from Federal Reserve System

Arthur W. Samansky, *Statfacts: Understanding Federal Reserve Statistical Reports,* Federal Reserve Bank of New York, November 1981.

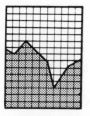

BUSINESS FAILURES

Business failures represent the number of companies that go out of business because of money owed to creditors. They include businesses which are closed due to court proceedings such as bankruptcy, foreclosure, and attachment or receivership, as well as those which were voluntarily closed either through compromises with creditors or by leaving unpaid debts. Failures exclude businesses which are closed due to causes such as lack of capital, inadequate profits, poor health or retirement of the owner, and change of name or location.

Where and When Available

Business failures measures are provided weekly, monthly, and quarterly by the Dun & Bradstreet Corporation. The figures are published in press releases and in the annual *Business Failure Record*.

The figures are available five days after the week to which they refer and two weeks after the month or quarter to which they refer. They are revised in subsequent weeks and months, and the annual revised figures are published in March of the following year.

Content

Business failures count the number of corporations and unincorporated businesses going out of business where a loss to creditors is involved. Information is provided on the dollar liabilities and age of the failed companies, causes of the failures, and the rate of failures (failures per 10,000 ongoing businesses). Additional detail on failures is provided by industry and by state.

The dollar liabilities reflect the debt at the time of the failure (the day the company closes operations). Liabilities include all accounts and notes payable and all obligations, whether or not secured, known to be held by banks, officers, affiliated companies, supplying companies, and governments. Liabilities exclude publicly-held bonds sold on securities exchanges. Assets are not used to offset liabilities in the data.

The business failures figures are not seasonally adjusted.

Methodology

Business failures data are obtained by Dun & Bradstreet reporters through checks of court records for bankruptcies, foreclosures, receivership, attachment, etc. Data for noncourt failures are obtained from local credit management groups and boards of trade, sales notices in newspapers, sheriff and auction sales, and personal contacts resulting from this monitoring. The figures are based on the universe count of all failures—samples are not used.

The failures data differ from the bankruptcy statistics of the Administrative Office of the U.S. Courts mainly because court figures are based on case numbers. In court proceedings, each partner is assigned a case number in contrast to the D & B grouping of all partners as one business failure. In addition, the D & B business failure data exclude some bankruptcies designated by the courts as business bankruptcies. The D & B assessments of court data find some court-designated business bankruptcies to be personal bankruptcies and find that some cases listed by the courts as a business were never actually in business.

The failure rate is calculated by dividing the number of failures by the number of firms which D & B classifies in its data base of all existing firms; this figure is then multiplied by 10,000 to obtain a rate of failure per 10,000 firms (the rate is expressed per

10,000 firms to insure that the relatively small number of failures in relation to all firms is a whole number). The data base excludes firms that are organized as a tax shelter, fledgling businesses that hope to become a going concern, and enterprises which are, in fact, persons moonlighting on second jobs to provide small additions to family income. Thus, it is smaller than the number of taxable firms in Internal Revenue Service statistics.

The D & B failure data were revised in 1984 by adding the following industries to the coverage: agriculture; forestry and fishing; finance, insurance, and real estate; and all services. Therefore, data prior to 1984 are not comparable (particularly relative to the level of business failures) to the subsequent years.

Accuracy

Because the failures figures are based on a universe count of firms, there are no measures of sampling error. Also, there are no estimates of revision error.

Relevance

Business failures indicate the ability of businesses, particularly small businesses, to withstand financial setbacks. When failures increase or are at relatively high levels, people are likely to be pessimistic about undertaking new enterprises (*business starts*). By contrast, when failures decline or are at low levels, a more conducive environment for small business is indicated.

Failures are related to business starts in previous years as well as to external and internal factors affecting the economic well-being of firms. Because business starts are risky ventures, an increasing number of starts leads to an increasing number of failures. Failures also result from external causes beyond the control of management, such as a slowly growing or declining *gross national product* and high *interest rates*, as well as from factors specific to the company, such as incompetent or inexperienced management, competition in product and local markets, expenses, and debt.

Recent Trends

Business failures declined during the late 1970s to an annual level of 7,000 companies in 1978. Failures subsequently rose through 1986, although the sharp increase from 1983 to 1984 reflected the change in methodology in 1984. Failures then leveled out at slightly over 60,000 in 1986 and 1987.

The failure rate in the 1980s was 4 to 5 times higher than the late 1970s, which, in part, reflects the greater number of *business starts* in the 1980s. Average liabilities per failure were in the

Table 7

Business Failures

	Number of firms (000)	Average liability per failure ($000)	Failure rate per 10,000 listed firms
1975	11	383	43
1976	10	313	35
1977	8	391	28
1978	7	401	24
1979	8	353	28
1980	12	395	42
1981	17	414	61
1982	25	627	88
1983	31	513	110
1984	52*	562	107
1985	57	645	115
1986	62	726	120
1987	61	594	102

Failures by Age of Business

	Total	3 years or less	4 to 5 years	6 to 10 years	Over 10 years
1986	100%	38.6	16.0	24.1	21.4
1987	100%	33.8	16.9	24.6	24.7

*Because of a change in methodology, the figures since 1984 are not comparable to those before 1984.

$400,000 range from 1975–81 and in the $600,000 range from 1982–87.

Many failures occur in relatively young firms. For example, in 1987, one-third of the failures were in firms zero to 3 years old and one-half of the failures were in firms zero to 5 years old.

Reference from Primary Data Source

The Dun & Bradstreet Corporation, *Business Failure Record,* annual.

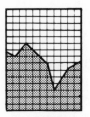

BUSINESS STARTS

Business starts represent the number of new businesses initiated. These business "births" include corporate and unincorporated for-profit businesses that are under independent ownership or are a subsidiary of an existing firm that was formed for expansion into a new line of business. They exclude previously existing companies that were reorganized through a change in ownership, a merger, or a shift between a corporate and noncorporate legal status, as well as firms that merely changed their name or location.

Where and When Available

Business starts measures are provided weekly, monthly, and quarterly by the Dun & Bradstreet Corporation. The figures are published in press releases and in the annual *Business Starts Record.*

The figures are available five days after the week to which they refer and two weeks after the month or quarter to which they refer. They are revised in subsequent weeks and annually in March of the following year.

Content

Business starts count the number of new businesses. No distinction is made in the count of starts for small, medium, or large-size businesses. However, information is provided on the total number of employees in the new companies and on the size distribution of new companies based on the number of employees. Additional detail on starts is provided by industry and by state.

A business is recognized as a start when a potential creditor asks Dun & Bradstreet for a credit rating on the firm. A new business is counted as a start in the year the credit rating request is made if it started operations within the last 36 months. This lag between the birth of the firm and its inclusion as a start is accepted as representing the time it takes the firm to be a going concern actively engaged in its line of business.

However, if a credit rating never is requested for a firm, the firm will never appear as a business start. If a credit rating is requested after three years from the birth, it also isn't included as a start, but it is included in the D & B data base of all existing firms. Because of exclusions of certain firms from the data base noted below under Methodology, the data base is smaller than the number of firms filing tax returns and accounted for in Internal Revenue Service statistics.

The business starts figures are not seasonally adjusted.

Methodology

The business starts data are based on a universe count of all new firms for which a credit rating request was received by the Dun & Bradstreet Corporation. No samples are used in this count.

The request for a credit rating is the sole source of information on the existence of a new business. This tends to exclude certain businesses from the starts statistics: those organized mainly as a tax shelter, fledgling businesses that hope to become a going concern, or persons moonlighting on second jobs that provide small additions to family income, as well as established businesses for which no credit rating request was made within three years of their birth.

The figures on starts since 1985 aren't comparable with those prior to 1985. The 1978–84 methodology counted a new business as a start only if a credit rating request for the firm was made in the same year as its birth. As noted above, the methodology instituted in 1985 counts a business as a start if the credit rating request is received within three years after the birth. Consequently, the number of starts is much higher since 1985.

Accuracy

Because the starts figures are based on a universe count of firms, there are no measures of sampling error. Also, there are no estimates of revision error.

Relevance

New businesses increase *employment* and *plant and equipment expenditures*. Increases in starts are associated with business confidence and willingness to take financial risks in pursuit of profits. Declines in starts indicates business people have a pessimistic outlook on profits and, therefore, are less willing to take financial risks.

Because business starts are risky ventures, an increasing number of starts leads to an increasing number of *business failures*. Some new ventures also borrow money for initial investments and start-up costs and, thus, are sensitive to the level of *interest rates* because of the dependence on *bank loans: commercial and industrial*.

In general, business starts are associated with the dynamism and entrepreneurial spirit in the economy. Most starts are small businesses which respond to a new demand or are the source of new products and new production technologies (which sometimes result in the receipt of patents for uniqueness of the invention).

Recent Trends

The data on business starts begin with 1978. As noted in the methodology, the figures on starts since 1985 aren't comparable with those before 1985. The new methodology included many more starts in 1985 than would have been counted under the old methodology.

Starts dropped from 119,000 in 1978 to around 90,000 during 1979–82 and then rose to just above 100,000 in 1983–84. In the figures based on the new methodology instituted in 1985, starts were in the 250,000 range in 1985–86 and then dropped to 234,000 in 1987.

The figures on employees per start probably aren't affected significantly by the 1985 change in methodology. The average number of employees in each start rose from 1978 to 1982 and then declined from 1982 to 1987. The typical level of employees per start declined from 6 workers during 1979–84 to 5 workers during 1985–87.

Table 8

Business Starts

	Firms (000)	Employees (000)	Employees per firm
1978	119	601	5.1
1979	88	499	5.7
1980	91	529	5.8
1981	92	565	6.1
1982	91	562	6.2
1983	101	607	6.0
1984	102	579	5.7
1985*	250	1,360	5.4
1986	253	1,226	4.8
1987	234	1,141	4.9

*Because of a change in methodology, figures since 1985 are not comparable to those before 1985.

Reference from Primary Data Source

The Dun & Bradstreet Corporation, *Business Starts Record*, annual.

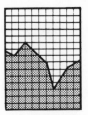

CAPACITY UTILIZATION

The capacity utilization rate (CUR) measures the proportion of plant and equipment capacity used in production by the manufacturing, mining, and electric and gas utilities industries. It covers the same industries as the *industrial production index*. When production rises faster than capacity, the CUR increases, but when production rises slower (or declines), the CUR decreases.

Where and When Available

The CUR is prepared monthly by the Federal Reserve Board. It is published in a press release and in the *Federal Reserve Bulletin*, the FRB's monthly magazine. Secondary sources include *Economic Indicators* and *Business Conditions Digest*.

The figures are available in the middle of the month after the month to which they refer, one day after the *industrial production index*. Preliminary data are provided for the preceding month; these are revised in the subsequent three months. Annual revisions are made in the fall.

Content

The CUR, expressed as a percent, is the ratio of the industrial production index to plant and equipment capacity. The formula is:

$$\text{CUR} = \frac{\text{Industrial Production Index}}{\text{Plant and Equipment Capacity}} \times 100$$

Because the numerator is discussed in the section on the production index, this section explains the denominator, or capacity.

The capacity figure represents the economy's ability to produce goods and power assuming the existing plant and equipment facilities are used over the normal operating period for each industry—this ranges from the 40-hour workweek to continuous operations seven days a week. Capacity gradually increases over time as more plant and equipment investment is added each year than physical capital is scrapped. This long-term upward trend shows no cyclical fluctuation. In contrast, industrial production is a highly volatile indictor over the course of the business cycle. As a result, CUR movements mirror the volatile movements of the production index.

The CUR figures are seasonally adjusted.

Methodology

Because the *industrial production index* is available monthly, the primary task for developing the CUR is to provide a measure of capacity. For most industries, direct measures of capacity, such as the number of items that can be produced if the industry is operating at a CUR of 100 percent, are not available. Consequently, indirect measures of capacity are widely used. These are typically derived from year-end surveys of capacity utilization conducted by McGraw-Hill, Inc., the Census Bureau, and other government and private sources. Capacity is inferred from these year-end CUR survey data by dividing these figures by the industrial production index for each industry. The resultant capacity figures are modified to reflect supplementary information on direct measures of capacity and on the value of stock of existing capital facilities. The monthly trends between these year-end levels of capacity are obtained by connecting the year-end points by a straight trend line. Monthly movements of the current year are extrapolated according to the monthly trend of the previous year.

Accuracy

The typical revision to the monthly CUR levels is plus or minus 0.3 percentage point.

Relevance

The CUR is used as an indicator of future plant and equipment investment spending. Generally, the higher the CUR, the greater the tendency for plant and equipment shortages to exist, which in turn leads to additional investment. However, it is important to analyze the CUR together with trends on business profits for clues to future investment. There is no specific CUR level which indicates a shortage of capacity or signals additional investment. Although the difference between 100 percent utilization and the CUR theoretically represents the unused capacity which is available to increase production to meet an increased demand, in fact, CURs typically don't top the 90th percentile except for selective industries such as paper, or during wartime when mobilization is high and less efficient facilities are put into production.

Rather, for some industries there are apparent CUR zones (typically ranging from the low to the mid-80s depending on the industry) which, if sustained over three or more years, are likely to be followed by additional plant and equipment investment. When CURs are below these zones, investment is mainly for replacing inefficient and outmoded facilities to reduce production costs rather than for increasing capacity to produce for expanding markets. Some examples of these zones are:

All manufacturing	80%
Electrical machinery	75%
Food	80%
Nonelectrical machinery	80%
Paper	85%
Electric and gas utilities	85%

For some industries, investment tends to follow the CUR movements of the previous year, such as chemicals and motor vehicles. In some industries, however, there is no apparent relationship between the CUR and investment, such as in petroleum refining.

Recent Trends

The CUR generally rose during the late 1970s and peaked in 1979 at 85–86 percent for manufacturing and utilities and in 1980 for mining at 93 percent. CURs then declined through 1983, particularly sharply for manufacturing and mining. Manufacturing partially rebounded in 1984 and then hovered around 80–81 percent during 1984–87. Mining and utilities also partially rebounded in 1984, but then generally declined during 1985–87.

From peak levels in the late 1970s, the manufacturing CUR during 1984–87 was 4 percentage points lower; the mining CUR

Table 9

**Capacity Utilization
(percent)**

	Total	Manufacturing	Mining	Utilities
1975	74.1%	72.3%	89.2%	84.3%
1976	78.8	77.4	89.7	85.3
1977	82.4	81.4	89.9	85.1
1978	84.8	84.2	90.3	85.0
1979	85.2	84.6	90.7	85.6
1980	80.9	79.3	93.2	85.4
1981	79.9	78.2	92.9	84.2
1982	72.1	70.3	83.4	81.4
1983	74.6	73.9	77.9	80.0
1984	81.0	80.5	84.0	83.0
1985	80.4	80.1	82.4	82.3
1986	79.4	79.7	76.4	79.1
1987	80.7	81.1	77.8	79.5

in 1987 was 15 percentage points below the 1970s' peak; and the utilities CUR was 6 percentage points less that year than during the 1970s peak. The total CUR for the three industry categories combined mirrored the patterns for manufacturing.

References from Primary Data Source

"Recent Developments in Economic Statistics at the Federal Reserve: Part 1," *Business Economics*, National Association of Business Economists, October 1988. This article was written by the staff of the Federal Reserve Board.

Richard D. Raddock, "Revised Federal Reserve Rates of Capacity Utilization," *Federal Reserve Bulletin*, October 1985.

Board of Governors of the Federal Reserve System, *Federal Reserve Measures of Capacity and Capacity Utilization*, 1978.

CAPITAL APPROPRIATIONS

Capital appropriations measure the designation of future expenditures for plant and equipment investment projects that have been approved by the responsible management body, such as the board of directors or the president of corporations. The figures cover appropriations for large manufacturing corporations. They include new appropriations which are made every quarter and the unspent backlog of appropriations made in previous periods.

Where and When Available

Measures of new capital appropriations and the unspent backlog are provided quarterly by the Conference Board. They are published in a press release and in the Conference Board's *Manufacturing Investment Statistics* (quarterly), *Manufacturing Investment Outlook* (quarterly), *Statistical Bulletin* (monthly), and *Across the Board* (monthly). Secondary sources include the *Business Conditions Digest*.

Historical quarterly data are available 70 days after the quarter to which they refer. The data are revised once in the quarter following their initial publication and annually for new seasonal factors. Annual projections of new capital appropriations and spending for the coming calendar year are published in December and revised the following April.

Content

The capital appropriations data are provided in both current and constant dollars. Measures of the unspent backlog of appropriations made in previous periods are available only in current dollars. Detailed data are shown for various durable and nondurable goods manufacturing industries.

Supplementary information is provided on the following factors: (1) how companies view the adequacy of their existing capital facilities capacity to produce products for their markets—"inadequate," "sufficient," or "more than adequate"; (2) the effect that current investment spending will have on existing capital capacity—"expansion," "no change," or "reduction"; (3) the extent to which shortages of raw materials or other goods obtained from suppliers outside the company affect production levels; and (4) the financing of future capital expenditures through funds internal or external to the company.

The capital appropriations figures are seasonally adjusted.

Methodology

Capital appropriations figures are based on a survey of the 1,000 largest manufacturing corporations. These companies had approximately 79 percent of all manufacturing corporate assets in 1985. The response rate to the survey is 65 percent of the weighted sample companies' assets. The constant dollar figures are calculated by dividing the current dollar data by the implicit price deflators for nonresidential fixed-investment structures and producers' durable equipment in the *gross national product*.

The figures on the unspent backlog of appropriations made in previous periods are derived from the following sequence:

	Opening backlog, beginning of quarter (end of previous quarter)
plus:	New appropriations during the quarter
minus:	Spending during the quarter
minus:	Cancellations during the quarter
equals:	Backlog, end of quarter

Accuracy

There are no estimates of sampling or revision error for the capital appropriations figures.

Relevance

Because appropriations occur before contracts for construction and orders for equipment are made, capital appropriations data give the earliest clue to future trends in spending for plant and equipment. However, appropriations are only a broad guide to future investment spending in the overall economy for two reasons. First, the appropriations data do not indicate when the spending will occur and second, the focus on the 1,000 largest manufacturing corporations limits coverage to about 30 percent of private nonfarm investment spending in all industries.

Table 10

Capital Appropriations of Large Manufacturing Corporations (billions of dollars)

	New appropriations		Unspent backlog, year-end (current dollars)
	(current dollars)	(1982 dollars)	
1975	45.4	77.7	46.4
1976	49.8	79.5	47.5
1977	63.9	96.0	56.5
1978	66.9	93.1	63.4
1979	88.0	113.0	76.5
1980	103.6	121.3	90.7
1981	105.5	113.1	92.5
1982	85.1	85.2	70.8
1983	88.0	88.7	73.5
1984	117.1	118.1	94.4
1985	108.9	107.9	94.6
1986	85.7	84.9	69.7
1987	119.2	119.9	78.1

Recent Trends

Appropriations showed volatile movements over the 1975–87 period. They rose during the late 1970s, except for a decline in the constant dollar figure in 1978. Following peaks in 1980 of $121 billion in constant dollars, appropriations during 1982 and 1983 dropped below levels of the late 1970s. After rebounding in 1984 to $118 billion, they declined sharply by 1986 and then recovered to $120 billion in 1987. These patterns generally were similar in the current dollar data.

The unspent backlog rose during the late 1970s to a high of $93 billion in 1981. The backlog dropped sharply in 1982 and, after recovering in 1984 and 1985 to $95 billion, the net effect of the sharp decline in 1986 and the increase in 1987 in appropriations was to leave the 1987 backlog at $78 billion.

Reference from Primary Data Source

The Conference Board, ''Presenting a New Series: A Quarterly Survey of Capital Appropriations,'' *Business Record*, October 1956.

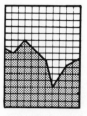

CONSUMER CONFIDENCE INDEX AND CONSUMER SENTIMENT INDEX

Two organizations provide indicators of consumer attitudes. They focus on consumer perceptions of general business conditions and of their personal financial well-being, plus their attitudes toward purchasing big-ticket items that last a relatively long time—homes, cars, furniture, and major household appliances. This section covers the overall indicators of both organizations: (1) the "consumer confidence index" of The Conference Board, and (2) the "consumer sentiment index" of The University of Michigan. Both indexes measure similar phenomena but, because the methodologies differ and the concepts aren't identical, there are periods when their movements differ. This section presents separate descriptions of the Conference Board and Michigan measures, summarizes the main differences between the two, and then analyzes the relevance and recent trends of both.

Consumer Confidence Index

The consumer confidence index (CCI) reflects consumers' attitudes toward the economy, local job markets, and their own financial condition.

Where and When Available

The CCI is provided monthly by the Consumer Research Center of The Conference Board. It is published in two Conference

Board monthly reports, the *Consumer Confidence Survey* and the *Statistical Bulletin*.

The CCI figures are available within the first five to ten days of the month after the month to which they refer. The data are revised for the previous month.

Content

The CCI represents the combined effects of household perceptions of general business conditions; perceptions of available jobs in the respondents' local areas currently and six months ahead; and expected personal family income six months ahead. A rising index means consumers are more optimistic, and a declining one signifies greater pessimism. There are no absolute values of optimism and pessimism, but comparisons of the index levels with previous periods indicate whether consumers are more optimistic or pessimistic than in past periods.

The CCI is based currently on 1985 = 100.

The CCI is seasonally adjusted.

Methodology

Data for the CCI are obtained from a monthly household survey conducted by National Family Opinion, Inc. for the Conference Board. The survey is mailed to approximately 5,000 households in the 48 mainland states and the District of Columbia, and the response rate is about 80 percent. A completely new group of households is surveyed each month.

The CCI is constructed by giving equal weight to each of five questions: two on local business conditions currently and six months ahead; two on jobs in the area currently and six months ahead; and one on personal family income six months ahead. In valuing the answers, positive responses are expressed as a percentage of the sum of the total positive and negative responses. Neutral answers are not counted. Depending on the question, positive answers are "good," "better," "plenty," "more," "higher"; negatives are "bad," "worse," "hard to get," "fewer," "lower"; and neutrals are "normal," "same," "not so many."

Accuracy

The sampling error in two out of three cases is approximately plus or minus 1.5 percentage points.

Consumer Sentiment Index

The consumer sentiment index (CSI) reflects consumer attitudes toward the economy, their own financial condition, and perceptions about buying big-ticket durable goods.

Where and When Available

The CSI is provided monthly by the Survey Research Center of The University of Michigan. It is published in the monthly report, *Surveys of Consumer Attitudes.* Secondary sources include the *Business Conditions Digest.*

The CSI figures are available within the first five to ten days of the month after the month to which they refer. The monthly data are not revised.

Content

The CSI combines three main categories of household attitudes toward the economy in one figure: (a) expected business conditions in the national economy for one and five years ahead, (b) personal financial well-being compared to one year earlier and expected one year later, and (c) whether the current period is a good or bad time to buy furniture and major household appliances. Upward movements of the index suggest that consumers are becoming more optimistic, and downward movements suggest a growing pessimism. While there are no absolute levels that define optimism and pessimism, comparisons of levels can be made between current and past periods. For example, the current period can be characterized as being more optimistic or pessimistic than past periods.

Supplementary information that can help in interpreting the reasons for changes in household attitudes is included in *Surveys of Consumer Attitudes*. The full report includes data on attitudes toward such items as employment, prices, interest rates, shortages, and government policies.

The CSI is based currently on 1966 = 100.

The CSI is not seasonally adjusted.

Methodology

Data for the CSI are obtained from a telephone survey of a sample of households conducted by the Survey Research Center. Approximately 500 households are contacted monthly in the 48 mainland states and the District of Columbia, with a response rate of about 80 percent. The sample is designed as a rotating panel in which one-half of the survey respondents is new each month and one-half is a carryover from the survey panel six months earlier.

There are five questions used in constructing the index. There are two questions on expected general economic conditions one year and five years ahead, two questions on personal financial well-being contrasting the current period with one year earlier and one year ahead, and one question on whether the current period is a good time to buy furniture and major household appliances. Equal weight is given to each question. In valuing the answers, only positive and negative replies are used. Depending on the question, positive answers are "up," "better," "good"; negatives are "down," "worse," "bad"; and neutrals are "same," "no change," "uncertain." The proportion of negative responses are subtracted from the proportion of the positive responses (of the sum of positives and negatives), and 100 is added to the difference to avoid negative numbers as follows:

$$\frac{\text{Positive}}{\text{Positive} + \text{Negative}} - \frac{\text{Negative}}{\text{Positive} + \text{Negative}} + 100$$

Accuracy

The sampling error for the CSI in two cases out of three is plus or minus 1.3 percentage points.

Main Differences between the Conference Board and Michigan Indexes

While the CCI and CSI indexes basically measure the same phenomena, there are clear differences in their methodologies associated with the index content, wording of questions, seasonal adjustment, household samples, data collection, and questionnaire response evaluation. The main differences are summarized below.

INDEX CONTENT. The CCI excludes the purchase of big-ticket items, while the CSI includes them.

WORDING OF QUESTIONS. For general business conditions, the CCI focuses on the respondent's local economy with a short-term current and six-month outlook, while the CSI focuses on the national economy and a long-term outlook of one to five years ahead. The CCI also includes questions on both current and expected job opportunities which are not in the CSI.

For personal financial well-being, the CCI looks at family income six months ahead, while the CSI asks how well-off the respondent is financially compared with one year earlier and what expectations are for one year ahead.

SEASONAL ADJUSTMENT. The CCI is seasonally adjusted, while the CSI is not seasonally adjusted.

MONTHLY HOUSEHOLD SAMPLE. The CCI sample is 5,000 households, while the CSI sample is 500 households.

DATA COLLECTION. The CCI uses a mail questionnaire, while the CSI uses a telephone interview.

SURVEY RESPONSE EVALUATION. The CCI AND CSI apply different weights for positive and negative answers to survey questions.

Relevance

Perceptions by households of the strength of general business conditions and of their personal financial conditions are closely linked to consumers' feelings of optimism and pessimism about the economy. In theory, when consumers are optimistic, they are more willing to increase spending and incur debt to finance the higher spending. When consumers are pessimistic, they are likely to cut back on spending, pay off debts, and build nestegg savings. An individual's decision to buy a home or other "big-ticket" durable goods is typically based on advance planning and is heavily influenced by consumers' perceptions of changing economic conditions.

When there are large changes in the indexes, the CCI and CSI are fairly good predictors of shifts in future consumer spending and saving; however, the actual levels of the indexes are less important as harbingers of future spending and saving.

The CCI is considered a leading indicator of economic activity according to Conference Board calculations. The CSI is classified as a leading indicator of economic activity by the Bureau of Economic Analysis in the U.S. Department of Commerce. (In addition, Michigan University's "index of consumer expectations," which is based only on the three questions in the CSI relating to the future [the CSI has five questions], is a component of the leading index of the *leading, coincident, and lagging indexes*.) Because the monthly and even quarterly movements show erratic increases and decreases, both indexes should be viewed over longer periods to discern a change from past trends.

Recent Trends

The CCI showed three different movements over the 1975–87 period. It declined from a peak of 106 in 1978 to 59 in 1982, then rose to 102 in 1984, and subsequently drifted down and then rebounded to 103 in 1987. The CSI showed three different movements over the 1975–87 period. It declined from a peak of 88 in 1977 to 68 in 1982, then rose to 98 in 1984, and subsequently declined to 91 in 1987.

Methodological differences between the two indexes result in variable monthly and longer period movements between the CCI and the CSI. The extent to which each methodological factor accounts for the varying movements is not quantifiable. Despite the methodological differences, however, the two indexes are conceptually similar. They challenge economic analysts when they show distinctly different movements for several months.

Table 11

Consumer Attitude Indexes

	Consumer confidence index (1985 = 100)	Consumer sentiment index (1966 = 100)
1975	74.5	70.4
1976	94.3	86.2
1977	97.9	87.7
1978	106.0	80.2
1979	91.9	66.0
1980	73.8	64.2
1981	77.4	70.0
1982	59.0	68.0
1983	85.7	87.5
1984	102.3	97.5
1985	100.0	93.2
1986	94.7	94.8
1987	102.6	90.6

References from Primary Data Sources

Fabian Linden, "The Consumer as Forecaster," *Public Opinion Quarterly*, Fall 1982.

Richard T. Curtin, "Indicators of Consumer Behavior: The University of Michigan Surveys of Consumers," *Public Opinion Quarterly*, Fall 1982.

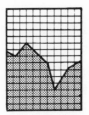

CONSUMER INSTALLMENT CREDIT

Consumer installment credit represents loans to households for financing consumer purchases of goods and services and for refinancing existing consumer debt. The loans are scheduled to be repaid in two or more monthly payments. Credit payable in one month or in a lump sum, such as charge accounts and single-payment loans, are excluded from the installment credit figures.

Where and When Available

Measures of consumer installment credit are provided monthly by the Federal Reserve Board. They are published in a statistical release and in the *Federal Reserve Bulletin*, the FRB's monthly magazine. Secondary sources include *Economic Indicators*, the *Survey of Current Business*, and *Business Conditions Digest*.

The figures are available approximately six weeks after the month to which they refer. The data are revised for the previous month and annually as part of a periodic benchmarking.

Content

The main categories of consumer credit are: auto (passenger cars and station wagons); revolving credit (credit cards used for sales transactions or for cash advances and check credit plans that allow overdrafts up to certain amounts on personal accounts); and "other" loans to consumers for items not specified in the above categories, such as home improvement, recreational vehicles, vans and pickup trucks, and student loans. Secured and unsecured loans are included, except those secured with real estate; loans secured with real estate, including home equity loans (which may be used for consumer spending), are defined as mortgage loans. Securitized consumer loans—loans made by finance companies, banks, and retailers that are sold as securities—are included.

The figures reflect consumer installment credit outstanding at the end of the month. The monthly change in consumer credit outstanding is the net effect of credit extensions and repayments during the month. Separate data on credit extended and repaid during the month are not available.

Methodology

Monthly data on consumer installment credit are based on the following: monthly surveys of a sample of commercial banks conducted by the Federal Reserve Board; monthly surveys of consumer finance companies, including auto finance companies, conducted by the Federal Reserve Board; monthly surveys of a sample of savings and loan associations conducted by the Federal Home Loan Bank Board; monthly surveys of credit unions conducted by the National Credit Union Administration (for federally insured credit unions) and by the Credit Union National Association (for other credit unions); and monthly surveys of retail sales conducted by the Bureau of the Census. Benchmark data are available annually for commercial banks, savings and loan associations, mutual savings banks, and retailers (accounts receivable), and every five years for finance companies.

Accuracy

There are no estimates of sampling or revision error for the consumer installment credit figures.

Relevance

Consumer installment credit supplements *personal income* as a source of consumer purchasing power. While consumer credit outstanding typically increases, the rate of increase is faster during expansions than recessions. The occasional monthly declines in consumer credit occur mostly during recessions. Thus, consumer credit accentuates the cyclical movements of consumer spending, particularly for durable goods. People generally borrow more during periods of rapidly growing personal income, because prosperity leads to optimism regarding financial commitments. Consumer installment credit is part of the business and consumer credit component of the leading index of the *leading, coincident, and lagging indexes.*

Existing consumer credit is also viewed as a burden on households because they must pay the principal and interest on the loans. The proportion of personal income that consumer credit represents is a commonly used measure of this burden. As this percentage rises during expansions, the growing consumer credit can be expected to depress further consumer borrowing. The

Table 12

Consumer Installment Credit Outstanding

	Credit outstanding (billions of dollars) December	Annual percent change Dec. to Dec.
1975	$167.0	3.0%
1976	187.8	12.5
1977	221.5	17.9
1978	262.0	18.3
1979	296.5	13.2
1980	297.6	0.4
1981	310.7	4.4
1982	323.5	4.1
1983	367.9	13.7
1984	442.5	20.3
1985	517.8	17.0
1986	571.8	10.4
1987	613.0	7.2

ratio of consumer installment credit outstanding to personal income is a component of the lagging index of the *leading, coincident, and lagging indexes*.

Recent Trends

Following a rapid increase in consumer credit during the late 1970s, the rate of growth dropped sharply during the recession years of 1980–82. After a substantial pickup in credit growth over 1983–85, a slowdown occurred in 1986–87. The rate of change in consumer credit is highly variable, reflecting the volatility of consumer spending for durable goods.

References from Primary Data Source

"Recent Developments in Economic Statistics at the Federal Reserve: Part 1," *Business Economics*, National Association of Business Economists, October 1988. This article was written by the staff of the Federal Reserve Board.

"Revisions to Consumer Installment Credit Series," *Federal Reserve statistical release*, Board of Governors of the Federal Reserve System, May 5, 1989.

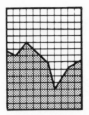

CONSUMER PRICE INDEX

The consumer price index (CPI) gauges the overall rate of price change for a fixed basket of goods and services bought by households. Because it prices the same items every month, this measure of inflation or deflation reflects the cost of maintaining the same purchases over time. The CPI is not a cost of living index since it does not measure the cost of living in absolute dollar levels. Rather, it focuses on percentage price changes of the items or services households frequently buy.

Where and When Available

The (CPI) is provided monthly by the Bureau of Labor Statistics in the U.S. Department of Labor. The data are published in a press release; in the BLS magazine, the *Monthly Labor Review*; and in *The CPI Detailed Report*. Secondary sources include *Economic Indicators*, the *Survey of Current Business*, *Business Conditions Digest*, and the *Federal Reserve Bulletin*.

The figures are published in the third or fourth week of the month immediately following the month to which they refer. They are not revised on a regular monthly basis. Major benchmark revisions are made approximately every ten years, mainly to reflect changes in the goods and services households buy. Smaller technical revisions, such as including or substituting new products or refining the methodology, are occasionally made between benchmarks.

Content

The CPI records price changes in food and beverages, housing, apparel, transportation, medical care, entertainment, education, personal care, and tobacco products. It is published in two versions, the CPI-U and the CPI-W. The CPI-U represents all urban households including urban workers in all occupations, the unemployed, and retired persons; in 1980, this accounted for 80 percent of the noninstitutional population. The CPI-W represents urban wage and clerical workers employed in blue-collar occupations; it accounted for 32 percent of the 1980 noninstitutional population. Both CPI measures exclude rural households, military personnel, and persons in institutionalized housing such as prisons, old age homes, and long-term hospital care.

CPIs are calculated for the nation as a whole, for broad geographic regions, and for large metropolitan areas. They therefore provide differential national and geographic measures of price movements. However, the CPI does not reflect the actual dollar level of living costs in the nation or in one area compared to another.

Rather, the weights of the CPI are based on the proportion of household income that consumers actually spend for particular goods and services. The CPI reflects actual spending patterns. It is not a "standard of living" concept which prices spending patterns aimed at achieving certain standards of nutrition, housing, health, etc., that society considers appropriate. The indicator measures price changes associated with buying the same set of items over periods of approximately ten years (the spending patterns are updated every ten years). Currently, the CPI is based on spending patterns during the 1982–84 period.

The CPI is based on actual transaction prices, which take into account such variations as premiums or discounts from the list price, sales and excise taxes, import duties, and trade-in allowances when the used car trade-in is part of the new car price. The CPI reflects price movements for the same or similar item exclusive of enhancement or reduction in the quality or quantity of the item.

The CPI is currently based on 1982–84 = 100.

The CPI figures are seasonally adjusted.

Methodology

The monthly price data are obtained from surveys of retail and service establishments, utilities, and households. Surveyors visit the same retail and service establishments and price the same items (or close substitutes) every month or bimonthly, depending on the city and item in the survey sample. To reduce survey costs, rental information is obtained by less frequent visits (every six months) to one of six groups of apartments and single family homes. The monthly rental price represents the weighted change of rentals for the most recent month and the prior six-month period for the same group of housing units. For example, the same groups are surveyed at six-month intervals for January and July, February and August, etc. Price data for electric utilities are obtained from mail surveys conducted by the U.S. Department of Energy.

The current index weights, which represent the proportion of household budgets spent on the various components, reflect consumer purchasing patterns during 1982–84. The weights are revised approximately every ten years based on surveys of households to determine their actual purchase patterns. These surveys also obtain information on which retail establishments that purchases are made, in order that greater weight may be given to prices in stores that have the largest sales volumes.

If the quality or quantity of an item in the monthly survey has changed, an adjustment is made to reflect the improvement or decline. The goal is to price products having the same functional characteristics over time. For example, if an apartment building is renovated to include air conditioning, the increased rent attributable to the air conditioning is not represented as a price increase in the CPI. By contrast, if a loaf of bread gets smaller but the price remains the same, the price of bread per unit has in fact increased and is represented as a price increase in the CPI. Because the data needed to make the necessary adjustments are not always available, the CPI contains an unknown amount of price change caused by quality and quantity changes.

Accuracy

Precise measures of the sampling error are not available for the CPI. As a broad order of magnitude, a change of at least 0.3 percent in the CPI over a one-month period or over several months is considered statistically significant.

Relevance

The CPI is the most widely quoted figure on inflation. In the formulation of fiscal and monetary policies (see Relevance under *gross national product*), trends in the CPI are a major guide in determining whether economic growth should be stimulated or restrained.

The CPI is also contrasted with *unemployment* to analyze the tradeoff between *inflation* and unemployment. (The concept that inflation and unemployment are inversely related is referred to as the Phillips Curve.) Maintaining a better balance between inflation and unemployment was included in the goals of the Full Employment and Balanced Growth Act of 1978 (Humphrey-Hawkins Act). The Act set a 1988 goal of zero percent inflation based on the CPI and 4 percent unemployment. In 1987, the CPI increased by 3.6 percent and the unemployment rate was 6.1 percent. Thus, greater reductions are required in inflation than in unemployment to reach the goals. The Act allows a deviation from the inflation goal if it impedes achieving the unemployment goal.

The CPI is used in a variety of ways to adjust for cost escalation in commerce and government programs: inflation adjustments to wages, pensions, and income maintenance payments for cost of living allowances; inflation adjustments in business contracts; and indexing of federal individual income tax returns to limit the inflation-induced bracket creep. Many labor-management union contracts are based on CPI-W. Businesses also trade CPI futures on the Coffee, Sugar, and Cocoa Exchange to hedge against future price changes. In addition, the CPI is used to deflate various economic indicators to reflect constant prices such as the *gross national product.*

Recent Trends

Inflation as reflected in the CPI-U accelerated sharply in the late 1970s, reaching a peak annual increase of 13.5 percent in 1980. Inflation then slowed during 1981–83 to a low of 3 percent in 1983. Subsequently, during 1984–87, inflation fluctuated in the 3

Table 13

**Consumer Price Index
(annual percent change)**

	CPI-U			CPI-W
	All items	All items excluding energy	All items excluding food and energy	All items
1975	9.1	8.9	9.1	9.1
1976	5.8	5.6	6.5	5.7
1977	6.5	6.4	6.3	6.5
1978	7.6	7.8	7.4	7.7
1979	11.3	10.0	9.8	11.4
1980	13.5	11.6	12.4	13.4
1981	10.3	10.0	10.4	10.3
1982	6.2	6.7	7.4	6.0
1983	3.2	3.6	4.0	3.0
1984	4.3	4.7	5.0	3.5
1985	3.6	3.9	4.3	3.5
1986	1.9	3.9	4.0	1.6
1987	3.6	4.1	4.1	3.6

to 4 percent range, although it declined to 2 percent in 1986 because of the sharp drop in oil prices in that year. Inflation rates based on the CPI-U and CPI-W are quite similar. Only occasionally do they differ by more than 0.2 percentage point on an annual basis.

Focusing on price changes excluding energy or excluding food and energy moderates the yearly fluctuations in the CPI during years when oil and food prices fluctuated sharply. (Price measures that exclude food and energy are referred to as the underlying rate of inflation—see *inflation*.) Over the 1975–87 period, the movements of the CPI excluding oil prices and oil and food prices differed from that for all items by 1 to 2 percentage points in 1979, 1980, and 1986.

References from Primary Data Source

Bureau of Labor Statistics, U.S. Department of Labor, *BLS Handbook of Methods*, April 1988, Chapter 19.

Bureau of Labor Statistics, U.S. Department of Labor, *The Consumer Price Index: 1987 Revision*, BLS Report 736, January 1987.

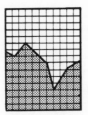

CRB FUTURES PRICE INDEX

The CRB Index represents futures prices of 21 raw and semi-processed commodities sold up to nine months in advance of delivery. These expected prices differ from actual prices when the futures contracts expire.

Where and When Available

The CRB Futures Price Index (CRB Index) is provided daily by the Commodity Research Bureau and the New York Futures Exchange, Inc. It is disseminated electronically by the New York Futures Exchange and published in the *Wall Street Journal* and *New York Times*. The New York Futures Exchange provides an up-to-date index every 15 seconds during trading hours.

Revisions are made when new commodities are added and existing ones deleted to reflect changing trading volumes.

Content

The 21 commodities and their general groupings in the index are: coffee, cocoa, and sugar (imports); live cattle, hogs, and pork bellies (meats); corn, oats, wheat, soybeans, soybean meal, and soybean oil (grains); crude oil, heating oil, copper, lumber, and cotton (industrials); gold, silver, and platinum (metals); and orange juice (miscellaneous). Separate indexes are developed for the broad components of imports, meats, grains, industrials, metals, and miscellaneous.

The CRB is currently based on 1967 = 100.

The CRB figures are not seasonally adjusted.

Methodology

Prices are based on actual sales (not bids and offers) of commodity futures on the various commodity exchanges. If the commodity isn't sold during the day, the closing price of the previous day is used in calculating the current day index.

The index construction uses both arithmetic and geometric averaging. Each commodity is weighted equally in the base year of the index. The calculation is made as follows: (1) to obtain the 1967 base period, futures prices in 1967 over nine months are averaged arithmetically for each of the 21 commodities; (2) these 21 arithmetic averages are averaged geometrically into a single 1967 base period figure, say A; (3) the same procedure of arithmetic and geometric averaging is done for futures prices in the current month, resulting in a single current month figure, say B; (4) the CRB Index is obtained by dividing B by A and multiplying by 100.

Geometric averaging insures that relatively large price increases or decreases for particular commodities do not influence the index more than items having small price changes (by contrast, the *consumer price index, producer price indexes, import and export price indexes,* and *GNP price indexes* are averaged arithmetically). Technically, arithmetic averaging is the sum of n numbers divided by n, and geometric averaging is the nth root of the product of n numbers.

Accuracy

There are no estimates of sampling or revision error for the CRB Index.

Relevance

The CRB Index is an indicator of future inflation because of its sensitivity to actual and perceived shortages and surpluses of the component commodities. The index movements are a precursor to movements in the crude materials index of the *producer price indexes* (the PPI represents current prices of a broader range of raw materials, and, as noted above under Methodology, the PPI movements are also averaged differently). Because raw materials and commodities in the early stage of processing become a decreasing component of the production cost of semifinished and finished goods, the CRB Index is of particular interest when it shows large price movements over sustained periods. These are more likely to have a subsequent, significant impact on semifinished and finished goods prices.

In addition, businesses trade CRB Index futures on the New York Futures Exchange to hedge against price changes.

Table 14

CRB Futures Price Index
(1967 = 100)

	December	Annual percent change (Dec. to Dec.)
1975	191.0	−6.3%
1976	204.7	7.2
1977	200.3	−2.1
1978	227.6	13.6
1979	281.5	23.7
1980	308.5	9.6
1981	254.9	−17.4
1982	234.0	−8.2
1983	277.6	18.6
1984	244.2	−12.0
1985	229.2	−6.0
1986	209.1	−8.8
1987	232.5	11.2

Recent Trends

The CRB Index has volatile price movements. Annual price changes from 1975 to 1987 show large price increases in one year and large price decreases in the following year, sharply accelerating and decelerating rates of inflation, and consecutive years of substantial price declines.

References from Primary Data Sources

New York Futures Exchange, Inc., *CRB Index Futures Reference Guide*, 1987.

Commodity Research Bureau, *The CRB Futures Price Index . . . A Glimpse at* Tomorrow . . . *Today,* 1988.

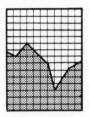

DISTRIBUTION OF INCOME

The distribution of income figures represent the proportion of total household income as received by households in low, middle, and high-income groups. The data are typically shown in quintiles, which array the number of households from the lowest to the highest fifths based on income. For example, in 1986, after the payment of income taxes, the 20 percent of households with the lowest incomes received 4 percent of all income, while the 20 percent of households with the highest incomes received 43 percent of all income. Quintile income groups (or quartiles for fourths, deciles for tenths, etc.) provide a relative measure of the change in income distribution over time by comparing the position of one income group to others. They do not indicate the absolute dollar income of each group. Dollar incomes generally rise over time because of higher *inflation* and *productivity*.

Where and When Available

The Bureau of the Census in the U.S. Department of Commerce provides annual measures of the distribution of income. The figures are published annually in *Household After-Tax Income* and *Money Income of Households, Families, and Persons in the United States*.

Before-tax measures are available in the summer after the year to which they refer. After-tax measures are available in the spring of the following year (the year after the before-tax figures). Revisions for previous years are made in the annual publications.

Content

The income measures represent household money income (cash income) both before and after the payment of income taxes, social security taxes, and property taxes. Money income is derived from wages, self-employment earnings, social security and other income maintenance benefits, interest, dividends, rent, and all other cash income that is regularly received. Noncash benefits such as food stamps, Medicare, Medicaid, and rent supplements, as well as income from nonrecurring sources such as capital gains and life insurance settlements, are excluded from money income.

Household income figures are categorized both before and after taxes by various dollar income ranges (e.g., under $2,500, $2,500–4,999 . . . $60,000–74,999, $75,000 and over), as well as by the quintile percentages. Additional detail on income before taxes is shown separately for families and unrelated individuals for the different dollar income groups; this detail is not provided for quintiles or on an after-tax basis. (A family refers to two or more persons related by blood, marriage, or adoption and living together in a house, apartment, or rooms intended for separate living quarters. A household consists of all families and unrelated individuals living together.)

Methodology

The basic before-tax income data are based on the current population survey (CPS) conducted by the Census Bureau. The information is collected every March for the previous calendar year. The survey sample is approximately 60,000 households. Typically, 57,000 are interviewed and 3,000 aren't available for interviews. For additional detail on the CPS, see *unemployment*.

Estimates of household income after taxes are based on tax simulations incorporating the CPS income figures with several other data sources. Federal and state income taxes are simulated based on data from the Internal Revenue Service's *Statistics of Income* and the Commerce Clearinghouse, Inc.'s *State Tax Handbook*; social security and federal retirement taxes are estimated using the legal percentage rates for these taxes; and property taxes are estimated from information in the U.S. Department of Housing and Urban Development's american housing survey.

Accuracy

The sampling error in 2 of 3 cases for the share of income before taxes is approximately 0.1 percentage point for the lowest quintile and 0.8 percentage point for the highest quintile. This differential reflects the greater proportion of income in the highest quintile.

Based on estimates derived from administrative records of the income tax, unemployment insurance, social security, and other programs, survey respondents tend to understate their income by approximately 10 percent in the aggregate for all sources of income. However, this overall underreporting isn't taken into account in developing the income distribution figures because determining the variations in underreporting among income groups is difficult.

Relevance

The income distribution focuses on differences in economic well-being among groups in the population. The data show how equitably income is distributed in society and highlight how overall economic trends are affecting different income groups. A large disparity in the distribution suggests a society that is divided into "haves" and "have nots," which raises both economic and social concerns. Economic growth is hindered when purchasing power and profit-motivated incentives are not broadly based. Socially, a large disparity results in increasing discord and despair among the population. Economic growth and social harmony are regarded as essential to a democratic and stable society,

Table 15

Distribution of Income: Households' Shares (percent)

Income Before Taxes	1987	1986	1985	1984	1983	1982	1981	1980	1974
Lowest fifth	3.8	3.7	3.9	4.0	3.9	4.0	4.0	4.1	4.2
Second fifth	9.6	9.7	9.7	9.8	9.9	9.9	10.0	10.2	10.6
Third fifth	16.1	16.2	16.3	16.4	16.4	16.5	16.7	16.8	17.1
Fourth fifth	24.4	24.3	24.4	24.6	24.6	24.6	24.8	24.8	24.6
Highest fifth	46.1	46.1	45.7	45.3	45.2	45.0	44.4	44.2	43.5
	100.0%	100.0%	100.0%	100.0%	100.0%	100.0%	100.0%	100.0%	100.0%

Income After Taxes	1987	1986	1985	1984	1983	1982	1981	1980	1974
Lowest fifth		4.4	4.6	4.7	4.7	4.7	4.9	4.9	4.9
Second fifth		10.9	11.0	11.0	11.1	11.3	11.5	11.6	11.7
Third fifth		17.2	17.2	17.2	17.4	17.5	17.8	17.9	17.8
Fourth fifth		24.8	24.7	24.8	24.8	24.8	25.0	25.1	24.7
Highest fifth		42.6	42.6	42.3	42.1	41.8	40.9	40.6	41.0
		100.0%	100.0%	100.0%	100.0%	100.0%	100.0%	100.0%	100.0%

even while political and economic philosophies for achieving these goals differ. Measures of *poverty* are related to the distribution of income.

Recent Trends

The quintile income distribution from 1980 to 1987 showed a declining proportion of income received in each of the first four fifths of households and an increasing proportion received by the top fifth. This pattern occurred both on a before-tax and an after-tax basis (figures after taxes go through 1986). Before taxes, the top fifth rose from receiving 44.2 percent of all income in 1980 to receiving 46.1 percent of all income in 1987 (1.9 percentage points). After taxes, the top fifth rose from 40.6 percent in 1980 to 42.6 percent in 1986 (2 percentage points).

After-tax income measures are available on a regular basis beginning in 1980, with earlier data for the single year of 1974. The figures show the 1974 distribution in comparison to 1980 to be slightly more equitable before taxes and little different after taxes.

References from Primary Data Source

Bureau of the Census, U.S. Department of Commerce, *Household After-Tax Income*, annual.

Bureau of the Census, U.S. Department of Commerce, *Money Income of Households, Families, and Persons in the United States*, annual.

EMPLOYMENT

Employment represents workers engaged in gainful work. There are two official measures of employment. One is a count of jobs and is detailed here. The other, which is a count of employed persons that is provided as part of the *unemployment* figures, is detailed in that section. The main differences in the two measures are summarized at the end of this section.

Where and When Available

Employment data are provided monthly by the Bureau of Labor Statistics in the U.S. Department of Labor. The data are published in a press release and in two BLS monthly magazines, the *Monthly Labor Review* and *Employment and Earnings*. Secondary sources include *Economic Indicators*, the *Survey of Current Business, Business Conditions Digest*, and the *Federal Reserve Bulletin*.

The monthly figures are available on the third Friday after the week containing the 12th of the month, which falls on the first or second Friday of the month following the month to which they refer. On the day the data are released, the Commissioner of Labor Statistics reports on recent employment and unemployment trends to the Joint Economic Committee of Congress. Preliminary data are provided for the immediately preceding month; these are revised in the subsequent two months. Annual revisions are made in June of the following year.

Content

Employment figures count the number of paid nonfarm civilian jobs. To be counted, a job must be on the payroll of a business, government, or nonprofit organization. Since some individuals hold two or more jobs, the number of jobs exceeds the number of working persons. Employment data exclude farm jobs, self-employment, domestic jobs in private households, unpaid family work, and the armed forces.

Persons on paid leave for illness or vacation are counted as employed because the job continues as a payroll cost. Those who are temporarily not working because of illness, vacation, strike, or lockout and who are not paid during this absence are not counted as employed.

The employment figures are seasonally adjusted.

Methodology

The employment data are based on employer payroll records that represent employees on payrolls during pay periods which include the 12th day of the month. The data are obtained from a mail survey of a sample of 310,000 employer establishments in 1988 that includes employers with only one work location as well as those with several establishments. The survey sample covered 40 percent of all nonfarm employment in 1987. The sample is weighted toward large establishments: large establishments are sure to be included in the sample while small establishments have less of a chance of inclusion. The survey sample is not a probability sample. The employment estimates are calculated for specific industries and categories of governments, and the figures for the industry and government components are summed to obtain the nonfarm economy-wide total.

The surveys of industry establishments and state and local governments are conducted for BLS by state employment agencies. Data covering all federal civilian workers are provided by the U.S. Office of Personnel Management. The monthly estimates are based on changes in employment by the same establishments reporting in the preceding month.

The monthly data are revised every year based on the universe of all employers that pay unemployment insurance premiums to state employment offices. These benchmark data are obtained for March of the previous year, and the relative revision for March is carried back through the previous eleven months and extrapolated forward to the current period.

Because of the difficulty of obtaining timely information on the startup of new firms, the payroll survey is late in capturing the employment of these firms. To compensate for this understatement of employment, the survey figures are augmented by an estimate of the additional employment generated by the new firms that have not yet been incorporated in the survey. The estimate is based on the difference between the benchmark and the sample survey data of the past three years and the relationship of the employment movement in the most recent quarter to the average employment growth over the past several years. If the current employment growth is smaller than the long-term rate, the survey figures are augmented by less-than-average additional employment for the undercoverage of new firms, and if the current employment growth is greater than the long-term rate, the survey figures are augmented by more-than-average additional employment for the undercoverage of new firms. The effect of this "bias adjustment" is to correct at an early stage for the delayed coverage of new firms and for the tendency of the sample to understate employment growth when the average size of the establishment in the industry is small.

Accuracy

The annual benchmark data typically revise employment levels within a range of plus or minus 0.5 percentage point. The average benchmark revision is 0.2 percentage point. Revisions in recent

years were under 0.05 percentage point in 1985, 0.5 percentage
point in 1986, and under 0.05 percentage point in 1987. Shorter-
term revisions in the monthly data show that in two of three
chances, the monthly level will be revised between plus or minus
110,000 (or 0.1 percent) between the preliminary figure and the
revision two months later, and the monthly change between plus
or minus 101,000 (or 50 percent of the typical month-to-month
movement).

Relevance

Employment is the main source of household incomes, which, in
turn, are spent on consumer goods and services. Because consumer spending accounts for approximately 65 percent of the
gross national product, employment is a key factor affecting
economic growth. In addition, employment is a component of the
coincident index of the *leading, coincident, and lagging indexes*.

The distribution of employment between high and low paying
jobs also affects household incomes. The types of jobs held influence economic growth as well as living conditions, because the
bulk of the population depends on employment for their major
source of income.

Recent Trends

Employment based on the payroll survey rose from 77 million in
1975 to 102 million in 1987, for an average annual increase of
2 million, equivalent to a compounded annual rate of 2.4 percent.
The compounded annual rate changed noticeably during the period. For example, employment rose by 4.2 percent during 1976–
79, declined by 0.4 percent during 1980–82, and rose by 3.2
percent during 1983–87. (Comparative trends in the payroll and
household surveys of employment are noted in the next section.)

Comparison of Alternative Employment Measures

This section summarizes the main differences between the employment figures obtained from surveys of employer payroll rec-

ords described in this section and the employment data associated with *unemployment* which are based on a household survey.

COVERAGE. Employment figures based on the payroll survey are limited to employees in nonagricultural industries and government civilian workers who are paid for their work or for their absence from the job. By contrast, employment figures based on the household survey cover a broader range of employment, including farm and nonfarm workers, the self-employed, government civilian workers and the U.S. resident armed forces, private household workers, unpaid workers in a family business, plus those temporarily absent from work due to illness, vacation, strike, or lockout, whether or not they are paid during their absence. The payroll figures partially compensate for their smaller coverage by including workers of all ages and multiple jobs of workers, while the household survey is limited to workers 16 years and older and counts each worker only once regardless of how many jobs they may hold. The net effect is that the household survey exceeds the payroll survey in 1987 by 10 million civilian workers and close to 12 million when the armed forces are included.

RECENT TRENDS. Both the payroll and the household surveys show similar long-term movements in employment. For example, over the 1975–87 period, payroll employment rose by 25.4 million for an annual compounded rate of 2.4 percent, and household employment rose by 26.6 million for an annual rate of 2.3 percent. Similarly, both surveys showed increases in employment in all years except 1982, although the decline in 1982 was noticeably sharper in the payroll survey (-2.0 percent in the payroll survey and -1.0 percent in the household survey).

Short-term monthly movements in the two surveys occasionally show different patterns over a few months, indicating a temporary uncertainty in the job figures. However, the payroll survey generally has significantly smaller month-to-month movements and, thus, a smoother short-term trend than the household survey. The smoother movement in the payroll survey results from three factors: (1) the payroll survey has a much larger sample of respondents; (2) employment associated with new firms that haven't yet been incorporated in the payroll survey sample, but for which an estimate is added every month to the survey figures, lessens the chance of an employment decline in the payroll survey; and (3) the payroll survey aims at maintaining all existing firms in the sample and getting firms that are in the sample design, but not reporting, to become active respondents, while the household survey rotates household respondents out of the survey and replaces them with new households to reduce reporting burden.

In absolute numbers, the household survey is significantly larger than the payroll survey—the differential rose from 9 million in the late 1970s to 10 million in the late 1980s.

ACCURACY. The payroll survey has a much larger sample than the household survey—310,000 business establishments accounting for 40 percent of payroll employment, compared to 60,000 households accounting for under 0.1 percent of household employment. However, the household survey has a more representative sample of survey respondents; it is a probability sample while the payroll survey sample is not. This allows for reliable estimates from a much smaller sample. The payroll survey may have less response error because it uses actual employer payroll tax records rather than the subjective responses of persons in the household survey.

Because of the differences in the methodologies, error estimates based on monthly movements between the two surveys are not comparable. The payroll survey only shows errors due to revision, while the household survey only shows errors due to sampling (monthly movements in 2 of 3 cases have a sampling error of 205,000 workers).

Although it is difficult to compare the quality of the two employment measures, the payroll survey is superior for gauging overall employment growth, since it counts each job held by a person. The smoother month-to-month change in employment in the payroll survey also makes it more useful for interpreting monthly employment trends.

COMPONENT DETAIL. The household survey details the age, sex, and race of workers and, consequently, is useful for analyzing the demographics of employment trends. Analogously, the payroll survey details the industry composition of jobs which is useful in analyses of the industrial structure of employment. Therefore, each measure has its particular uses because of the different detail provided.

Table 16

**Alternative Employment Measures
(millions)**

	Payroll survey (nonfarm jobs)	Household survey (civilian workers)
1975	76.9	85.8
1976	79.4	88.8
1977	82.5	92.0
1978	86.7	96.0
1979	89.8	98.8
1980	90.4	99.3
1981	91.2	100.4
1982	89.6	99.5
1983	90.2	100.8
1984	94.5	105.0
1985	97.5	107.2
1986	99.5	109.6
1987	102.3	112.4

References from Primary Data Source

Bureau of Labor Statistics, U.S. Department of Labor, *BLS Handbook of Methods*, April 1988, Chapter 2.

Harvey R. Hamel and John T. Tucker, "Implementing the Levitan Commission recommendations to improve labor data," *Monthly Labor Review*, February 1985, pp. 20–22.

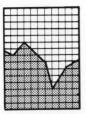

EMPLOYMENT COST INDEX

The employment cost index (ECI) measures changes in labor costs for money wages and salaries and noncash fringe benefits in nonfarm private industry and state and local governments for workers at all levels of responsibility. The ECI is not affected by shifts in the composition of employment between high wage and low wage industries or between high and low wage occupations within industries. Thus, the ECI represents labor costs for the same jobs over time.

(Another measure of employment costs is provided in the *Average Hourly Earnings Index*. This earnings index was replaced in 1989 by an expansion of the ECI to include more specific industries and occupational groups.)

Where and When Available

The employment cost index (ECI) is provided quarterly by the Bureau of Labor Statistics in the U.S. Department of Labor. The data are published in a press release and in two BLS monthly magazines, the *Monthly Labor Review* and *Current Wage Developments*.

The figures are available during the last week of the month immediately following the quarter to which they refer (April for the first quarter, July for the second quarter, November for the third quarter, and February for the fourth quarter). No revisions are made in subsequent quarters.

Content

The ECI figures include money wages and salaries, fringe benefit paid leave for vacations, illness, holidays, etc., commissions,
bonuses, and noncash health, retirement, and other fringe benefits in private nonfarm industries and in state and local governments. Costs are included for all workers—production, nonsupervisory, supervisory, and executive. The wage and salary
component of labor costs reflects straight-time pay only, excluding premium rates for overtime, holidays, night work, and hazardous conditions. The fringe benefit component reflects changes
in the cost of existing benefits, such as higher pay for holidays, as
well as changes in the provision of benefits, such as an additional
paid holiday.

The ECI represents a fixed composition of industries and of
occupations within industries. Therefore, movements over time
are not affected by shifts between higher and lower paying industries and occupations. In addition to industry and occupational
detail, the index distinguishes wage costs between union and
nonunion workers. The index was started in 1976 based on wages
and salaries and was expanded in 1979 to include noncash fringe
benefits. Wages and salaries plus fringe benefits are called compensation.

The ECI is currently based on an index base of 1981 = 100.
Beginning in 1990, the ECI will be based on June 1989 = 100.

The ECI figures are not seasonally adjusted.

Methodology

The ECI data are based on a survey of employer payrolls in the
third month of the quarter (March, June, September, and December) for the pay period including the 12th day of the month. The
survey is a probability sample of approximately 3,600 private
industry employers and 700 state and local governments, public
schools, and public hospitals.

The index weights represent the wage and fringe benefit costs
of each occupation within an industry. This is average wage and
fringe benefits per worker multiplied by the number of workers in

each occupation/industry group. The employment data are obtained from the census of population and the wage and fringe benefit data are from the ECI survey. Until June 1986, the fixed composition of industry and occupational employment was based on the distributions from the 1970 census of population. Since then, the composition reflects the distributions of the 1980 population census. In contrast to the overall ECI, the component indexes for union and nonunion workers are based on current period distributions rather than fixed weights because of the changing union status of workers within a company.

Accuracy

In two of three cases, the 12-month percent change in the ECI for private industry workers is statistically significant within a range of plus or minus 0.23 percentage point, and in 19 of 20 cases the range is plus or minus 0.46 percentage point. For state and local government workers, in two of three cases the range is plus or minus 0.28 percentage point and in 19 of 20 cases it is plus or minus 0.56 percentage point.

Relevance

The ECI is the most comprehensive and refined measure of underlying trends in employee compensation as a cost of production. It is used for analyzing changes in wages and fringe benefits in relation to *productivity* and *inflation*, as a guide in collective bargaining negotiations, and for cost escalators in union and other business contracts. In distinguishing between union and nonunion workers, it also provides data for contrasting wage trends between collective bargaining and unorganized companies.

Recent Trends

The ECI for compensation (money wages plus fringe benefits) increased at a declining rate during the 1980s. For private industry workers, the increases of 10 percent in 1980–81 slowed to 3 percent in 1986–87. This deceleration was sharper for union workers than for nonunion workers. Annual percent increases were larger for union workers during 1980–83, while nonunion workers had larger increases during 1984–87. State and local government workers had larger percent increases than private industry workers during 1982–87.

Table 17

**Employment Cost Index: Compensation
(annual percent change)**

	Private industry workers	Private union workers	Private nonunion workers	State & local government workers
December				
1980	9.8%	11.1%	8.9%	NA
1981	9.8	10.7	9.4	NA
1982	6.4	7.2	6.0	7.2%
1983	5.7	5.8	5.7	6.0
1984	4.9	4.3	5.2	6.6
1985	3.9	2.6	4.6	5.7
1986	3.2	2.1	3.6	5.2
1987	3.3	2.8	3.6	4.4

NA: Not available

References from Primary Data Source

Bureau of Labor Statistics, U.S. Department of Labor, *BLS Handbook of Methods*, April 1988, Chapter 8.

C. Donald Wood, "Employment Cost Index series to replace Hourly Earnings Index," *Monthly Labor Review*, July 1988.

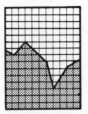

FARM PARITY RATIO

The farm parity ratio is a crude measure of changes in farmers' purchasing power. Purchasing power reflects the relationship between (a) the prices farmers receive for sales of crop and livestock products, and (b) the prices farmers pay for production and living expenses. This relationship is a limited measure of the change in purchasing power because it doesn't include the effects of improvements in production technology or of the changing quantities and quality of farm products sold. The 1910–14 period is used as the base for comparison because prices of farm and nonfarm items were considered to have been generally in balance in that period by the legislators who passed the Agricultural Adjustment Act of 1939 establishing the parity ratio.

Where and When Available

The farm parity ratio is provided quarterly by the National Agricultural Statistics Service of the U.S. Department of Agriculture. It is published in a press release and in the report, *Agricultural Prices*. Secondary sources include *Economic Indicators* and the *Survey of Current Business*.

The figures are available one month after the quarter to which they refer (the end of January, April, July, and October). Revisions are made quarterly, and annually in January of the following year.

Content

The farm parity ratio is composed of the index of prices received for sales of crop and livestock products in the numerator, and the index of prices paid for farm production and living expenses in the denominator. The percent change in both indexes reflects the movement from 1910–14 to the current period. Currently, the ratio using 1977 = 100 is also provided to facilitate comparisons with other price indexes. Basing the ratio on 1977 does not affect percent changes from one period to another, but the number levels are different. Thus, when using the 1977 base, a comparison with 1910–14 isn't readily observable unless back data are shown for the earlier period. When either ratio is above 100, farmers' purchasing power is higher than in the base period, and when either ratio is below 100, their purchasing power is less than in the base period.

The current weights in both the prices received and the prices paid indexes reflect the relative dollar importance of sales and expenses of the components of each index during 1971–73. In the prices received index, crops account for 44 percent of the weight and livestock products for 56 percent. Crop products include food and feed grains, cotton, tobacco, oil bearing crops (e.g., soybeans and peanuts), and fruits and vegetables. Livestock products include meat animals, dairy products, poultry, and eggs. The index represents about 90 percent of the cash receipts from all farm products: of the excluded commodities, livestock products such as wool, horses, goats, and ducks account for 2 percent and crop products such as forest, nursery, greenhouse, and specialty crops account for 8 percent.

In the prices paid index, farm production expenses are weighted 70 percent and living expenses are weighted 30 percent. Farm production costs include such items as feed, feeder livestock, seed, fertilizer, fuels, chemicals, equipment, cash rent, wages, interest, and real estate taxes. The living expense component is based on the *consumer price index* (CPI-U).

The farm parity ratio is currently based both on 1910–1914 = 100 and 1977 = 100.

The farm parity ratio figures are not seasonally adjusted.

Methodology

Weights for the prices received and prices paid indexes are changed at intervals of several years with no set pattern. The current weights are based on the importance of the components during 1971–73. Prior to this, weights were based on the 1953–57 period.

Data for the prices received index are based on U.S. Department of Agriculture surveys of marketings and prices for various crop and livestock products. Similar data sources are used for the base period weights and the current period prices. The prices received data are not adjusted for changes in the quality of the farm products.

Data for the prices paid index are developed from different sources for the weights and the current period prices. The weights are based on U.S. Department of Agriculture annual surveys of farm production expenditures during 1971–73 for the production component of the index, and on a Department of Agriculture 1973 survey of farm family living expenditures. Current period prices are derived from surveys of firms that sell to farmers and in some cases directly from farmers, the *consumer price index*, and a Department of Agriculture quarterly survey of farm labor wage rates. Since 1986, prices paid data are developed only for the first month of the quarter. The prices paid data for farm expenditures are not adjusted for changes in the quality of the goods and services bought; the living expense component of prices paid is adjusted for changes in quality in the *consumer price index*.

Accuracy

There are no estimates of sampling or revision error for the farm parity ratio.

Relevance

The farm parity ratio is a broad indicator of the economic well-being of farmers. Because the ratio does not reflect improvements in farm production technology or changes in the quantity and quality of farm products sold, it is not an indicator of farm income. However, it gives a clue as to whether price movements are more or less favorable to farmers and, thus, provides an early indication of a change in income for farmers. Used with projections of the production of crop and livestock products, it provides a rough indication of the likely magnitude of changes in income. In addition, by focusing attention on the price component of income, the farm parity ratio may also influence the nature of farm price support laws.

Table 18

Farm Parity Ratio
(1977 = 100)

	Farm parity ratio	Prices received index	Prices paid index
1975	113	101	89
1976	107	102	95
1977	100	100	100
1978	106	115	108
1979	107	132	123
1980	97	134	138
1981	92	139	150
1982	84	133	159
1983	84	135	161
1984	86	142	165
1985	79	128	163
1986	77	123	159
1987	78	127	162

Recent Trends

The parity ratio declined over the 1975–87 period, in general. Although there were a few years of minor increase, the basic thrust was downward. From an average of 106 in the late 1970s, the ratio fell to an average of 78 between 1985 and 1987 (1977 = 100).

Reference from Primary Data Source

Statistical Reporting Service, U.S. Department of Agriculture, *Scope and Methods of the Statistical Reporting Service*, September 1983.

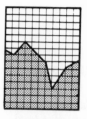

FLOW OF FUNDS

The flow of funds measures are a financial and economic accounting system of the sources and uses of money and credit and of the financial assets and liabilities of households, businesses, governments, and foreigners (in their economic activities in the U.S. economy). The system relates the *gross national product* to the lending, borrowing, and investment funds used in financing the nation's output. It also shows the debt in the private and public sectors of the economy.

Where and When Available

The flow of funds measures are provided quarterly by the Federal Reserve Board. They are published in a statistical release and in the *Federal Reserve Bulletin*, the FRB's monthly magazine. Secondary sources include *Economic Indicators*.

The figures are available two months after the quarter to which they refer. The data are revised quarterly and annually to reflect more complete information.

Content

The flow of funds represents sources and uses of money, credit, and equity funds. Conceptually, the totals of all sources and uses are equal. There are two main sources of funds: (1) wage, profit, interest, and rent income generated in the production of goods and services, and (2) credit such as mortgages, bonds, bank loans, consumer credit, trade credit, and commercial paper, plus corporate stock (equity capital). Income derived from production is an ''internal'' source of funds, while credit and corporate stock are ''external'' sources that require raising funds in the marketplace and, thus, are sensitive to interest rates. The uses of funds include spending for consumer goods and services; savings in bank deposits and in life insurance and pension reserves; and investment in plant and equipment, housing, inventories, and financial assets.

Asset and liability figures are shown for bank deposits, life insurance and pension reserves, mortgages, bank loans, other credit, and corporate stock. The data on debt refer to money owed on borrowings for mortgages, bonds, bank loans, consumer credit, and commercial paper.

The flow of funds figures are seasonally adjusted.

Methodology

The flow of funds figures are based on many data sources for the financial elements, plus the *gross national product* for the income and product flows that are available monthly or quarterly, and on trend estimates for those elements that are available less frequently. The annual revisions incorporate the GNP revisions.

Accuracy

There are no estimates of sampling or revision error for the flow of funds measures.

Relevance

The flow of funds measures are used to assess funding requirements associated with varying rates of economic growth and inflation. The Federal Reserve Board uses the measures as a guide in evaluating the needs and availability of money and credit to influence the *money supply* and *interest rates* through monetary policy. Funding requirements are included in projections of the *gross national product* and *inflation* to make more realistic forecasts. The flow of funds measures help to reconcile assumed growth in spending (GNP) and supply constraints (inflation) with the availability of money, credit, and equity funds. The flow of funds is also the source of quarterly debt figures.

Contrary to other economic indicators, the flow of funds mea-

Table 19

Flow of Funds (illustrative): Net Funds Raised
(billions of dollars)

	1985	1986	1987
Domestic nonfinancial borrowing			
Borrowing sectors	631.1	616.7	543.9
Households	293.4	281.1	245.6
Corporate	166.7	190.2	172.6
Nonfarm noncorporate	93.1	116.2	102.5
Farm	−13.9	−15.1	−10.0
State & local governments	91.8	44.3	33.3
Borrowing instruments	631.1	616.7	543.9
Consumer credit	94.6	65.8	30.1
Mortgages	237.7	300.6	299.8
Corporate bonds	73.8	121.3	125.4
Tax-exempt obligations	136.4	30.8	31.3
Bank loans (unclassified)	38.6	66.5	14.2
Open market paper	14.6	−9.3	2.3
Other	35.5	41.0	40.8
U.S. Government borrowing	223.6	215.0	141.4
Net foreign borrowing in U.S.	1.2	9.0	3.1
Corporate equity funds raised by nonfinancial corporations (new share issues)	−81.5	−80.8	−76.5

sures are not an economic barometer in their own right. That is, annual increases or decreases are not the focus of attention, and therefore there is no section below on Recent Trends. The flow of funds data are significant because they provide an integrated statistical system for measuring borrowing and lending in analyses of monetary policies and financial markets.

References from Primary Data Source

"Recent Developments in Economic Statistics at the Federal Reserve: Part 2," *Business Economics*, National Association of Business Economists, July 1989. This article was written by the staff of the Federal Reserve Board.

Board of Governors of the Federal Reserve System, *Introduction to Flow of Funds*, 1980.

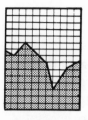

GNP PRICE MEASURES

There are three measures of price change associated with the *gross national product*: implicit price deflator, chain price index, and fixed-weighted price index. The three GNP price measures are the most comprehensive indicators of price change of the American economy. They include the goods and services elements of consumer, investment, government, and international economic transactions in the GNP. Because of the different methodologies used in their calculation, the three measures result in alternative trends in prices. In doing so, they provide a basis for addressing the innate problem of index number construction discussed in the Introduction.

Where and When Available

The three GNP price measures are provided quarterly by the Bureau of Economic Analysis in the U.S. Department of Commerce. The data are published in a monthly press release and in BEA's monthly magazine, the *Survey of Current Business*. Secondary sources include *Economic Indicators*, *Business Conditions Digest*, and the *Monthly Labor Review*.

The figures are available during the third or fourth week of every month. Preliminary data for the immediately preceding quarter are provided in the month following the quarter (April for the first quarter, July for the second quarter, etc.). These are initially revised in the subsequent two months. More detailed revisions are made annually every July, and comprehensive benchmark revisions are published about every five years.

Content

The three GNP price measures are developed for the entire GNP and for the consumer, investment, government, and international components. The three measures vary in the composition of the goods and services items covered.

The IMPLICIT PRICE DEFLATOR represents the changing distribution of goods and services bought in the marketplace in every period. It includes the effect on overall price movements of the continually changing allocation of resources among the GNP components and changing preferences for goods and services consumption items within a component. For example, if there is a shift in spending within the consumer component from food to medical care, and medical care prices increase more than food prices, the implicit price deflator will rise more sharply than the other measures because of the greater spending for medical care.

The CHAIN PRICE INDEX weights prices according to the goods and services item composition of the GNP for the last two consecutive quarters and annually for the last two consecutive years. Thus, the item composition is constant for two consecutive periods.

The FIXED-WEIGHTED PRICE INDEX weights price changes according to the composition of the goods and services items in the last GNP benchmark revision, thus holding the composition constant since the most recent benchmark. Benchmark revisions are made every five years. The historical data reflect these five-year periods between changes in the item composition. However, because of the time required to complete benchmarking, the current composition may be unchanged for up to 13 years after the most recent benchmarking. The most recent weights for the fixed-weighted price index reflect the GNP spending patterns in 1982.

The fixed-weighted price index and the chain price index are more direct measures of price change than the implicit price deflator. The fixed-weighted index and the chain price index focus sharply on price movements exclusive of the changing composition of purchased goods and services. By contrast, the implicit price deflator reflects both price changes and the changing composition of goods and services purchased.

The GNP price measures are currently based on 1982 = 100.

The GNP price measures are seasonally adjusted.

Methodology

All three measures are developed by using the price movements indicated mainly in the *consumer price index, producer price indexes*, and the *import and export price indexes*. These are supplemented with several other indexes, including those for construction costs and defense and computer prices. The IMPLICIT PRICE DEFLATOR is calculated by dividing current-dollar GNP by constant-dollar GNP. Since it is a byproduct of the estimation of GNP in constant dollars, it does not involve the conventional index number construction of multiplying price movements by the weights and summing the products as used in calculating the fixed-weighted and chain price indexes. Weights for the CHAIN PRICE INDEX and the FIXED-WEIGHTED PRICE INDEX are based on the GNP expenditure patterns discussed above in the Content section.

Accuracy

There are no estimates of sampling or revision error for the GNP price measures.

Relevance

The inclusion of all components of the economy in these three indexes is a unique feature of the GNP price measures. It enables comprehensive analyses of the sources of *inflation* in the consum-

er, investment, government, and international components integrated in a statistically consistent framework.

The alternatively weighted indexes allow flexibility in analyzing price movements. Depending on the particular analysis, one
index may be more appropriate than the others. However, in the
absence of a clear preference for a particular weighting scheme to
assess price change, the three measures together can be a realistic
compromise to the index number dilemma. Together, the three
yield a range for price movements and establish the upper and
lower bounds within which the true rate of price change lies (see
the section on index numbers in the Introduction).

In analyzing consumer price movements, it is also useful to
compare the movements of the GNP fixed-weighted index for
consumer expenditures to the *consumer price index*. Both indexes
are conceptually similar in terms of the constant weighting
scheme. However, there are two technical differences: the goods
and services items aren't identical, and the weights of the GNP
index represent spending of all consumers while the CPI weights
refer only to spending by urban civilian households. For example,
life insurance is included in the GNP index but excluded from the
CPI; private elementary, secondary, and college tuition but not
public college tuition are in the GNP index, while all private and
public tuition are in the CPI; and the GNP weights include rural
and military households that are excluded from the CPI. These
technical differences result in different movements that provide
an upper and lower bound in estimating consumer price movements; this range can supplement the above noted bounds in the
consumer components of three GNP price indexes.

Recent Trends

Inflation in the three GNP price indexes showed similar patterns over the 1975–87 period. Price increases accelerated during 1976–81 to a peak of 9.5 percent in 1981 (average of the
three indexes). Inflation then decelerated in 1982 and 1983 and
subsequently hovered around 3 to 4 percent during 1984–87,

although it fell below 3 percent in 1986.

Theoretically, for price movements after the most recent benchmarked base period, the implicit price deflator would be expected to show the lowest rate of inflation and the fixed-weighted price index the highest rate, with the chain price index between the two; in contrast, before the base period benchmark, the implicit price deflator would be expected to show the highest rate of inflation and the fixed-weighted price index the lowest. This reflects the effect of changing the weights for the fixed-weighted and chain price indexes with every benchmark. In practice, this expected result was borne out during 1975–87. From 1975–82, the implicit price deflator had the highest rate of inflation and the fixed-weighted price index had the lowest rate. These patterns reversed during 1983–87, when the implicit price deflator had the lowest inflation rate and the fixed-weighted price index had the highest.

Table 20

GNP Price Measures
(annual percent change)

	Implicit price deflator	Chain price index	Fixed-weighted price index
1975	9.8%	9.2%	8.0%
1976	6.4	5.9	5.3
1977	6.7	6.1	5.1
1978	7.3	7.2	6.2
1979	8.9	8.7	8.5
1980	9.0	9.0	9.3
1981	9.7	9.4	9.3
1982	6.4	6.3	6.2
1983	3.9	4.1	4.1
1984	3.7	3.9	4.0
1985	3.0	3.3	3.4
1986	2.7	2.5	2.8
1987	3.3	3.4	3.6

References from Primary Data Source

Bureau of Economic Analysis, U.S. Department of Commerce, *The National Income and Product Accounts of the United States, 1929–82: Statistical Tables*, September 1986, p. xiii.

Carol S. Carson, "GNP: An Overview of Source Data and Estimating Methods," *Survey of Current Business*, July 1987.

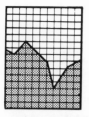

GOVERNMENT BUDGETS AND DEBT

Measures of government budgets represent spending and revenue for all levels of government—federal, state, and local. Spending and revenues are based, in part, on legislation appropriating funds to be spent and on tax laws specifying what items are to be taxed and the taxation rates. Actual spending and revenue are also influenced by the state of the economy. The budget is in balance when spending equals revenue, in surplus when revenue exceeds spending, and in deficit when spending exceeds revenue. There are two measures of government spending and revenue which are based on different concepts: one is based on the official budget and the other is based on statistical definitions of the national income and product accounts.

Government debt is a result of borrowing. Much of the debt represents the cumulative excess of annual budget deficits over annual budget surpluses in previous years, less the debt that has been paid off. In addition, some borrowing occurs in anticipation of spending in future years, particularly for capital construction projects of state and local governments.

Where and When Available

The U.S. Office of Management and Budget publishes annual figures on the official federal budget in the *Budget of the United States Government*. The U.S. Department of the Treasury publishes monthly data on the federal budget in the *Monthly Treasury Statement of Receipts and Outlays of the United States Government*. The Bureau of Economic Analysis in the U.S. Department of Commerce publishes quarterly statistical measures of budgets of the federal government and of the total of all state and local governments in a press release and in BEA's monthly magazine, the *Survey of Current Business*. The Bureau of the Census in the U.S. Department of Commerce publishes annual data on all governments—federal, state, and local—in a press release and in *Government Finances*. Secondary sources include *Economic Indicators*, the *Federal Reserve Bulletin*, and *Business Conditions Digest*.

The official OMB federal budget figures are available every January when the President submits the budget to Congress. The Treasury figures are available three or four weeks after the month to which they refer; they are revised continuously during the year. The BEA statistical budgets are available in the month after the quarter (April for the first quarter, July for the second quarter, etc.); they are revised in the following quarter, with subsequent revisions made annually every July, and comprehensive benchmark revisions made about every five years. The Census Bureau annual statistical budgets are available one year after the year to which they refer.

Content

Government spending represents government outlays for wages and fringe benefits of government workers; purchases of materials, equipment, structures, and services from private industry; and transfer payments to individuals, state and local governments, and business. Transfers include social security, unemployment insurance, food stamps, and other income maintenance programs; grants-in-aid to state and local governments; interest on the public debt; and subsidies to business. Government revenues encompass government receipts from income, sales, and property taxes; customs duties; and fees, licenses, and other miscellaneous sources of income.

The main components of spending and revenue differ between the federal government and state and local governments. For example, only the federal government spends for defense, social security, and farm subsidies, and collects customs duties; only state and local governments spend for local schools and police (although financed in part with federal grants-in-aid), and collect sales and property taxes.

OFFICIAL AND STATISTICAL BUDGETS

There are two measures of budgets. The official budget represents the legally recognized spending, revenues, and surplus or deficit that are used by governments in establishing actual figures. The statistical budget is consistent with the definitions of the national income and product accounts (NIPA), which conform to the concepts of the *gross national product*. (As noted below, there is another version of a statistical budget for state and local governments.) Differences in both item content and timing distinguish the official budget from the statistical budget.

The statistical budgets in the NIPA for the federal government and for state and local governments are seasonally adjusted. The monthly figures on the official federal budget are not seasonally adjusted. The Census state and local governments statistical budgets are annual figures and therefore are not seasonally adjusted.

DIFFERENCES IN ITEM CONTENT. For the FEDERAL government, examples of differences in item content between the official budget of the U.S. Office of Management and Budget and the NIPA statistical budget are: new loans and repayment of government loans are included in the official budget but excluded in the statistical budget; purchases and sales of land are included in the official budget but excluded in the statistical budget; government contributions to federal worker retirement funds are excluded in the official budget but included in the statistical budget; and spending and revenues in U.S. territories outside the

United States and the Commonwealth of Puerto Rico are included in the official budget but excluded in the statistical budget.

The official federal budget distinguishes between "on-budget" and "off-budget" items. All items are on-budget except social security funds for retirement and disability insurance. Because the off-budget items impact the economy, they are presented here as a combined total with on-budget items. By contrast, the statistical budget does not distinguish between on-budget and off-budget items.

For STATE AND LOCAL governments, there is no official budget total that combines all state and local budgets. However, there are two measures of statistical budgets. One is the NIPA budget and the other is the Census Bureau budget in *Government Finances*. The most significant differences in item content between these two statistical measures are: unemployment insurance payments and revenues are included in the Census budget but excluded in the NIPA budget (unemployment insurance is in the federal NIPA budget); purchases and sales of land are included in the Census budget but excluded in the NIPA budget; and government contributions to employee retirement funds are excluded in the Census budget but included in the NIPA budget.

DIFFERENCES IN TIMING. The timing differences reflect distinctions among the cash, accrual, and delivery methods of accounting. The cash basis counts spending when governments' payment checks are issued and revenues when taxpayers' checks are received. The accrual basis counts spending when the expense is incurred; similarly, accrued tax revenues are counted when tax liabilities are incurred. The delivery basis counts spending when the purchased items are delivered to the government.

The FEDERAL official budget is on a cash basis, except for payment of interest on the public debt which is on an accrual basis. The statistical budget is also on a cash basis, but with several exceptions. The primary exceptions are: for spending, payment of interest on the public debt is on an accrual basis, and payment for large defense items such as airplanes, missiles, and ships are recorded on a delivery basis; and for revenues, business income taxes are recorded on an accrual basis.

The two STATE AND LOCAL statistical budgets are mainly on a cash basis. The Census Bureau figures are completely on a cash basis. The NIPA figures are on a cash basis, except for interest payments and business income taxes which are on an accrual basis.

DEBT

Government debt represents short-term and long-term interest bearing obligations such as notes, bonds, and mortgages. It excludes non-interest bearing obligations (with minor exceptions), rights of individuals to government employee retirement funds, financial obligations of trust funds, and advances and contingent loans from other governments. It is included in the Office of Management and Budget official budget and in the Census Bureau statistical budgets, but not in the NIPA statistical budgets.

There are two measures of federal government debt. One is gross debt and the other is debt held by the public. GROSS DEBT is the total debt and includes securities owned by individuals, businesses, pension funds, and foreigners, as well as those owned by government funds. Government funds include two main types: trust funds such as social security, federal worker retirement, unemployment insurance, highway trust funds, and public enterprise "federal" funds such as the Postal Service, Overseas Private Investment Corporation, and the nuclear waste funds. DEBT HELD BY THE PUBLIC is confined to securities owned by individuals, businesses, pension funds, and foreigners, but excludes security holdings of federal funds. The government funds invest their balances in government securities as a source of interest income.

Methodology

Official budget figures for the FEDERAL government are based on reports of government agencies to the Office of Management and Budget and the Treasury Department. The Bureau of Economic

Analysis estimates the accrual and delivery-based elements for the NIPA budgets.

The annual NIPA figures for STATE AND LOCAL governments are based on Census Bureau surveys of all state governments and a sample of local governments that provide spending and revenue information on a yearly basis. The quarterly NIPA figures are based on survey data of the Bureau of Labor Statistics and the Census Bureau for payrolls, construction, and taxes and are supplemented by the trend of less recent actual data for the other components. The Bureau of Labor Statistics conducts a monthly survey of state and local government worker payrolls, and the Census Bureau conducts a monthly survey of state and local government-owned new construction and a quarterly survey of state and local tax revenues. The quarterly tax revenue figures are used in the historical NIPA measures but are too late for use in the current NIPA figures. The Bureau of Economic Analysis estimates the accrual elements for the NIPA budgets.

Accuracy

There are no estimates of sampling or revision error in government budgets. There is an estimate of sampling error in the Census Bureau state and local statistical budgets. This sampling error is based entirely on the local government component because all state governments are surveyed. (Local governments accounted for 60 percent of state and local spending and 56 percent of state and local revenues in 1987, exclusive of intergovernmental state payments to local governments.) In two of three cases, the local government sampling error is less than one-half of one percent.

Estimates of revision error in the NIPA measures are available only for the "purchases" component of total spending. For the federal government, the average revision error in the quarterly change in purchases, without regard to sign, is approximately 7 percentage points. For state and local government, the average revison error in purchases is 1.5 percentage points.

Relevance

BUDGETS

The official and statistical government budgets have different analytic uses. The federal official budget is better for assessing trends in spending, revenues, surpluses and deficits associated with spending appropriations, and tax legislation. The federal and the state and local statistical budgets are better for analyzing the relationship between the budget on the one hand and spending in the entire economy and economic growth on the other.

A budget surplus or deficit affects spending in the entire economy both directly and indirectly. The direct effect of a surplus (or reduction in the deficit) is to remove money from the income stream and, thus, restrain spending, although not necessarily proportionately; similarly, the direct effect of a deficit (or reduction in the surplus) is to add money to the income stream and, thereby, stimulate spending, although not necessarily proportionately.

The budget also affects spending indirectly through *interest rates*. These effects are in opposition to the more direct effects. Because a surplus (or reduction in the deficit) will reduce the debt (or slow down the increase in the debt), it will tend to lower interest rates and, consequently, stimulate spending; similarly, a deficit (or reduction in the surplus) will increase debt (or slow down the reduction in debt), resulting in higher interest rates which should restrain spending. The net result of these contrasting direct and indirect effects determines the overall impact of government budgets on the economy.

In addition to the budget impacting the economy, the economy impacts the budget through feedback effects. Because economic growth (measured by the *gross national product*) affects tax revenues and spending for unemployment insurance, periods of high economic growth generally tend toward a budget surplus and low growth periods tend toward a deficit.

The size and components of spending and revenue also influence the economy. The amount of total spending, as well as the specific amounts spent on the defense and civilian components, impact the nature of government services, *employment*, and the *distribution of income*. The amount of total revenue, as well as the specific amounts from component income, and sales and property taxes, affect business and employment incentives and the distribution of income.

DEBT

Government debt also affects *interest rates* through the sale of new securities and refinancing of existing debt in bond markets. A large debt provides substantial low-risk investment outlets as an alternative avenue for investing funds. During periods of considerable economic uncertainty, investment funds may be channeled toward government securities, resulting in higher interest rates for household and business borrowers.

Generally, debt held by the public is more relevant than gross debt for assessing the impact of debt on interest rates. The publicly held debt directly affects credit markets and bank reserves, while the government funds that are invested in gross debt are internal to the government and, thus, do not directly affect credit markets and bank reserves.

Recent Trends

BUDGETS

The federal budget changed significantly from the late 1970s to the 1980s. Following a steady decline in the annual deficit from $69 billion in 1975 to $16 billion in 1979, the deficit rose persistently to $206 billion in 1986 and then declined to $157 billion in 1987 (based on the NIPA statistical budget). State and local government budgets were in surplus over the entire 1975–87 period. The surplus rose continuously from the late 1970s to a peak of $65 billion in 1984, followed by a general decline to $53 billion in 1987.

Yearly differences between the official and statistical budgets fluctuate in regard to the federal deficit and, from 1984 through 1987, there was a complete turnaround in the difference. Thus, the federal deficit in the official budget exceeded that in the statistical budget by $20 to $22 billion in 1984 and 1985, the difference narrowed to $8 billion in 1986, and the official deficit was $13 billion lower than the statistical deficit in 1987. Because these differences are difficult to predict, there is always some uncertainty in relating the official budget to the statistical budget.

DEBT

Gross government debt rose noticeably more for the federal budget than for state and local budgets during 1975–87. Federal debt increased from $544 billion in 1975 to $2.35 trillion in 1987 (331 percent), based on the official budget; state and local debt rose from $221 billion in 1975 to $719 billion in 1987 (225 percent), based on statistical budgets. The state and local debt primarily results from advance borrowing for future government capital outlays, which more than offsets the continual annual budget surpluses. In addition, part of the state and local debt represents public debt for private purposes. Many state and local governments finance economic development by selling government bonds because of their lower interest rates (which reflect the federal tax exemption for interest income on these bonds). However, this debt is repaid by the private borrowers.

Over the 1975–87 period, federal debt held by the public rose more than gross debt, 376 percent to 331 percent. Publicly held debt (which excludes government funds) accounted for 80 percent of gross debt in 1987, up from 73 percent in 1975. Trust funds account for the dominant share of government funds—95 percent in 1988.

Table 21

Government Budgets and Debt
(billions of dollars)

Statistical Budgets

Calendar year	Federal			State and local		
	Revenue	Spending	Surplus, deficit (−)	Revenue	Spending	Surplus, deficit (−)
1975	294.9	364.2	−69.4	239.6	235.2	4.5
1976	340.1	393.7	−53.4	270.1	254.9	15.2
1977	384.1	430.1	−46.0	300.1	273.2	26.9
1978	441.4	470.7	−29.3	330.3	301.3	28.9
1979	505.0	521.1	−16.1	355.3	327.7	27.6
1980	553.8	615.1	−61.3	390.0	363.2	26.8
1981	639.5	703.3	−63.8	425.6	391.4	34.1
1982	635.3	781.2	−145.9	449.4	414.3	35.1
1983	659.9	835.9	−176.0	487.7	440.2	47.5
1984	726.0	895.6	−169.6	540.5	475.9	64.6
1985	788.7	985.6	−196.9	581.8	516.7	65.1
1986	828.3	1,033.9	−205.6	623.0	561.9	61.2
1987	916.5	1,074.2	−157.8	655.7	602.8	52.9

Comparison of Federal Official and Statistical Budget Deficit
(billions of dollars)

Fiscal year	Official	Statistical	Difference
1984	−185.3	−165.0	−20.3
1985	−212.3	−190.7	−21.6
1986	−221.2	−212.8	−8.4
1987	−150.4	−163.5	13.1

Government Debt
(billions of dollars)

End of fiscal year	Federal gross debt	Federal debt held by the public	State and local gross debt
1975	544.1	396.9	221.2
1980	914.3	715.1	336.6
1985	1,827.5	1,509.9	568.6
1986	2,120.1	1,736.2	658.9
1987	2,345.6	1,888.1	718.7

References from Primary Data Sources

U.S. Office of Management and Budget, Executive Office of the President, "Special Analysis B: Federal Transactions in the National Income and Product Accounts" and "Special Analysis E: Borrowing and Debt," *Budget of the United States Government*, Fiscal Year 1989, February 18, 1988.

Bureau of the Census, U.S. Department of Commerce, *Government Finances in 1986–87*, November 1988.

Bureau of Economic Analysis, U.S. Department of Commerce, *Government Transactions*, Methodology Paper Series MP-5, November 1988.

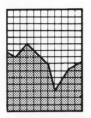

GROSS NATIONAL PRODUCT

The gross national product (GNP) is the broadest indicator of economic output and growth. It covers the goods and services produced and consumed in the private, public, domestic, and international sectors of the economy. Two measures of the GNP are provided, one from the viewpoint of demand that shows the markets for goods and services, and the other from the viewpoint of supply, showing the resource costs in producing the goods and services.

In addition, the GNP is presented in two ways with respect to price levels: in current dollars which represent actual prices in every period and in constant dollars which abstract from changing prices over time. The current-dollar GNP is the market value of goods and services produced. The constant-dollar GNP, which is referred to as real GNP, represents the quantity of economic output and is the measure used to define the rate of economic growth. Actual indicators of price movements are provided for the total GNP and its major components (*GNP price measures*).

Where and When Available

The GNP is provided quarterly by the Bureau of Economic Analysis in the U.S. Department of Commerce. The data are published in a monthly press release and in BEA's monthly magazine, the *Survey of Current Business*. Secondary sources include

Economic Indicators, the *Federal Reserve Bulletin*, and *Business Conditions Digest*.

The figures are available during the third or fourth week of every month. Initial (referred to as "advance") data are provided in the month after the quarter to which they refer (April for the first quarter, July for the second quarter, etc.); these are revised in the subsequent two months, with more detailed revisions made annually every July, and still more comprehensive benchmark revisions made about every five years.

Content

The composition of the two GNP measures is shown in Table 22. The "product side" reflects the demand or markets for goods and services, and the "income side" reflects the supply or costs of producing the goods and services. The two measures are conceptually equal, but they differ statistically because of inadequacies in the data; this difference is called the "statistical discrepancy."

GNP is measured on a "value added" basis. Only the value that is added in each stage of production from raw materials to semi-finished goods to final products is counted. This prevents endless double counting which would occur if goods and services purchased from other business for use in production were included.

The GNP figures are seasonally adjusted.

Product Side:
Demand Components

The component markets for the nation's output represent the demand aspects of the economy and are referred to as the product side of GNP. The product side total is the official GNP measure. It has the following main categories:

PERSONAL CONSUMPTION EXPENDITURES represent spending by households for durable goods, nondurables, and services and spending by nonprofit organizations for operating expenses.

Table 22

Gross National Product and Major Components, 1987

Product side

	$ billions	percent
Gross national product	4,526.7	100.0%
Personal consumption expenditures	3,012.1	66.5
Durable goods	421.9	9.3
Nondurable goods	997.9	22.0
Services	1,592.3	35.2
Gross private domestic investment	712.9	15.7
Nonresidential[a]	446.8	9.9
Residential[b]	226.9	5.0
Inventory change	39.2	0.9
Net exports	−123.0	−2.7
Exports	428.0	9.5
Imports	551.1	−12.2
Government purchases	924.7	20.4
Federal	382.0	8.4
State and local	542.8	12.0

Income side

	$ billions	percent
Gross national product	4,526.7	100.0%
Compensation of employees	2,683.4	59.3
Wages and salaries	2,248.4	49.7
Supplements	435.0	9.6
Proprietors' income[c]	312.9	6.9
Farm	43.0	0.9
Nonfarm	270.0	6.0
Rental income	18.4	0.4
Corporate profits	310.4	6.9
Net interest	353.6	7.8
Indirect business taxes[d]	366.3	8.1
Capital consumption allowances[e]	480.0	10.6
Business transfers, government subsidies, and government enterprises	9.8	0.2
Statistical discrepancy	−8.1	−0.2

Notes: Detail may not add to totals due to rounding.

[a]Business plant and equipment.
[b]Mainly new housing construction.
[c]Profits of unincorporated business.
[d]Mainly sales and property taxes.
[e]Mainly depreciation allowances.

GROSS PRIVATE DOMESTIC INVESTMENT represents business spending for equipment and nonresidential structures by for-profit and nonprofit organizations; residential construction; and the change in business inventories, excluding profit or loss, due to cost changes between the time of purchase and sale of inventoried goods.

GOVERNMENT PURCHASES OF GOODS AND SERVICES represent the federal, state, and local wages of government workers and purchases of civilian and defense goods and services, exclusive of transfer payments. (Total government spending which also includes social security and other income maintenance payments, federal grants to state governments and state grants to local governments, interest on the public debt, and subsidy payments to business is covered in *government budgets and debt*.)

NET EXPORTS OF GOODS AND SERVICES represent the international balance of exports minus imports in goods and services, including the balance of U.S. income from investments in companies and securities abroad less that of foreigners' income from investments in the United States.

Income Side:
Supply Components

The labor, capital, and tax costs in producing the nation's output are reflected in the supply aspects of the economy and is referred to as the income side of GNP. It has the following main categories:

COMPENSATION OF EMPLOYEES represents the money and in-kind wages and fringe benefits of workers.

PROPRIETORS' INCOME AND CORPORATE PROFITS represent business profits of unincorporated businesses and corporations, excluding the profit or loss due to cost changes between the time of acquisition and time of sales of inventories or to cost changes in replacing existing capital facilities since their acquisition.

RENTAL INCOME OF PERSONS represents profits to residential

and nonresidential real property owners who are not primarily engaged in real estate business, including nonmarket imputations of profits for owner-occupied housing as if such housing were rented at the market price, and royalties paid by businesses to individuals.

CAPITAL CONSUMPTION ALLOWANCES represent the depreciation allowances for the use of capital equipment and structures that are deducted as costs on business income tax returns and also are calculated for owner-occupied housing, including adjustments for the changing costs of replacing existing capital facilities from their original purchase cost.

INDIRECT BUSINESS TAXES represent sales and property taxes, customs duties, user fees, fines, and other analogous sources of government revenue.

Other Summary GNP Measures

In addition to the conventional GNP, several variants of total GNP are provided to assist in economic analysis. These are based on adjustments related to inventories, international transactions, and statistical problems. The most widely cited one is FINAL SALES, which excludes the effect of inventory increases or decreases. This results in highlighting underlying demand as represented by purchases of goods and services by households, business, government, or foreigners, independent of whether the highly volatile business inventories in stores, warehouses, and factories are accumulating or depleting. Other summary measures are final sales to domestic purchasers, gross domestic purchases, gross domestic product, and command GNP. Typically, the largest difference in the quarterly and annual movements between the conventional GNP and the other measures occurs in the case of final sales.

Methodology

The GNP is calculated using secondary data that are initially compiled for other purposes, which limits control of the quality of the data for GNP requirements. Because of this dependence on secondary data, BEA directs considerable attention to unusual movements in the data base and raises questions with the organizations providing primary data to determine if errors or special circumstances affect the figures. This close probing is done when the GNP components are first estimated and also repeated a second time when the total product and income sides are compared, particularly if there is a large difference (statistical discrepancy) between the two GNP aggregates. This process sometimes uncovers data problems that in turn lead to changing certain components to mitigate the problems. In addition, special formulas are used to adjust inventories and depreciation to exclude profit or loss due to changing costs of inventories or capital facilities between the time of purchase and their sale or replacement. These are referred to as the "inventory valuation adjustment" and "capital consumption adjustment," which are included in the product side under inventory change and in the income side under proprietors' income, corporate profits, and capital consumption allowance components.

The data used in constructing the GNP come from many government agencies and private organizations that provide statistics obtained from surveys, income tax returns, and regulatory reports. The items in this data base vary considerably in definition, collection technique, and timeliness and, thus, are of uneven quality. Because the two measures of GNP on the product and income sides are developed independently from different data sources, the statistical discrepancy between the two GNP totals indicates the extent of the inconsistency in the two data bases. Formally, the statistical discrepancy is the product side minus the income side.

Accuracy

There are no estimates of sampling error for the GNP figures. The statistical discrepancy indicates the extent to which unknown errors in the data bases, in which some are above and others below the "correct" values, do not cancel each other. However, because some of these errors are offsetting, the statistical discrepancy is a net figure of the consistency of the data bases rather than a gross measure of all errors regardless of whether the high and low figures are offsetting. As noted earlier, the product side GNP is regarded as the official measure, although the availability of the product and income sides allows the calculation of alternative growth rates that provide a lower and upper range for use in analysis (by comparing movements of the product side against the product side minus the statistical discrepancy). Thus, one way of viewing the accuracy of the GNP figures is to treat it as being within the growth rate range indicated by the product and income sides movements.

Another perspective on GNP accuracy is provided by considering the size of the revisions to provisional GNP figures. These are shown in terms of the confidence that the percentage growth rates in GNP and prices are likely to be revised upward or downward within a specified range based on past experience. For example, the growth rate of the estimate of the constant-dollar GNP that is published in the third month after the quarter to which it refers is revised in the succeeding annual revisions each July as follows: in 2 of 3 cases in a range of -1.8 to $+1.9$ percentage points and in 9 of 10 cases in a range of -2.7 to $+3.5$ percentage points.

Relevance

The GNP provides the overall framework for analyzing and forecasting economic trends. It has the unique attribute of integrating the markets for goods and services (demand or spending) with production of the goods and services (supply or costs) in one format. Because the costs of production also generate wage and profit incomes, the GNP measures provide the basis for analyzing the feedback effects between spending and incomes from one period to the next. The analyses are used to assist the President and Congress in formulating fiscal and incomes policies and the Federal Reserve Board in formulating monetary policies which are aimed at maximizing employment growth and minimizing inflation. Fiscal policies are enacted through federal spending and taxes (*government budgets and debt*), monetary policies through the *money supply* and *interest rates*, and incomes policies through price and wage voluntary guidelines and mandatory controls. Analyses of the cyclical expansion and recession movements and of the longer-term periods that span several cycles can suggest the likely future implications of adopting particular policies for moderating cyclical fluctuations and stimulating noninflationary long-term economic growth. The GNP is the main framework of such analyses, although it is supplemented by and integrated with data from other indicators.

Recent Trends

Real GNP increased in 10 of the 13 years over the 1975–87 period, with declines occurring in 1975, 1980, and 1982. Following annual increases averaging 5 percent during 1976–78, real GNP growth slowed during 1979–82 to increases of 2 to 2.5 percent in two years and decreases in the other two years. During 1983–87, real GNP rose 3.5 percent in three years with variations of almost 7 percent in 1984 and under 3 percent in 1986.

Table 23

Gross National Product

	Current dollars (billions)	1982 dollars (billions)	1982 dollars (percent change)
1975	1,598.4	2,695.0	−1.3%
1976	1,782.8	2,826.7	4.9
1977	1,990.5	2,958.6	4.7
1978	2,249.7	3,115.2	5.3
1979	2,508.2	3,192.4	2.5
1980	2,732.0	3,187.1	−0.2
1981	3,052.6	3,248.8	1.9
1982	3,166.0	3,166.0	−2.5
1983	3,405.7	3,279.1	3.6
1984	3,772.2	3,501.4	6.8
1985	4,014.9	3,618.7	3.4
1986	4,240.3	3,721.7	2.8
1987	4,526.7	3,847.0	3.4

References from Primary Data Source

Carol S. Carson, "GNP: An Overview of Source Data and Estimating Methods," *Survey of Current Business*, July 1987.

Allan H. Young, "Evaluation of the GNP Estimates," *Survey of Current Business*, August 1987.

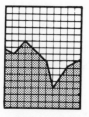

HELP-WANTED ADVERTISING INDEX

The help-wanted advertising index tracks employers' advertisements for job openings in the classified section of newspapers in 51 labor market areas. The index represents job vacancies resulting from turnover in existing positions such as workers changing jobs or retiring and from the creation of new jobs. It excludes nonadvertised job vacancies and jobs advertised in nonclassified sections of newspapers such as display ads in business or news sections.

Where and When Available

Measures of the help-wanted advertising index are provided monthly by The Conference Board. The figures are published in a press release and in the Conference Board's monthly *Statistical Bulletin*. Secondary sources include *Business Conditions Digest*.

The figures are available about 35 days after the month to which they refer. The data are revised in the following month.

Content

The help-wanted advertising figures cover jobs in many fields—professional, technical, crafts, office, sales, farm, custodial, etc. They include a higher proportion of all junior and middle level vacancies than managerial, executive, or unskilled levels. In addition to the national help-wanted index, local indexes for 51 labor markets are provided.

The index is currently based on 1967 = 100.

The help-wanted figures are seasonally adjusted.

Methodology

The help-wanted advertising figures are obtained from classified advertisements in one daily (including Sunday) newspaper in each of 51 labor markets (51 cities including their suburbs). Newspapers are selected according to how well their ads represent jobs in the local labor market area. The labor markets accounted for approximately one-half of nonagricultural employment in 1987.

The index reflects the number of job advertisements. Each advertisement is weighted equally regardless of whether it is an ad for one job or for multiple positions or whether for full-time or part-time work. Advertisements of both employers and employment agencies and advertisements for the same job on successive days are included in the count.

Index weights for the 51 labor markets are based on the proportion of nonagricultural *employment* accounted for by each of the labor markets. These weights are updated every two years. Within each market area, help-wanted advertisements in the Sunday newspaper are weighted according to the ratio of the average Sunday advertising volume to average daily advertising volume.

Accuracy

There are no estimates of sampling or revision error for the help-wanted advertising figures.

Relevance

The help-wanted advertising index indicates the direction of employers' hiring plans. In theory, it provides an advance signal of future changes in *employment* and cyclical turning points. In practice, the help-wanted index leads the downturn from the expansion peak to a recession, but it lags the turning point in moving from recession to expansion, based on analyses conducted as part of the *leading, coincident, and lagging indexes*. The lag in timing as the economy is recovering from a recession results from the tendency of employers to increase *average weekly hours* of existing workers when business improves or to call back workers on layoff before advertising for new workers.

The help-wanted index is inversely related to *unemployment*. When help-wanted advertisements increase, unemployment declines, while a decline in help-wanted advertisements is accompanied by a rise in unemployment. The help-wanted movements sometimes are sharper than the unemployment movements because of changing advertising practices. For example, during periods of low unemployment, employers may rely more heavily on help-wanted advertisements than on alternative means of finding workers. During high unemployment, employers may find

Table 24

Help-wanted Advertising Index
(1967 = 100)

1975	80
1976	95
1977	118
1978	149
1979	157
1980	128
1981	118
1982	86
1983	95
1984	130
1985	138
1986	138
1987	153

workers more easily through alternative means such as through workers initiating the contact on their own or on the advice of a friend.

Some advertised jobs may not be filled because employers are not satisfied with the applicants, there is an overall shortage of applicants, or employers decide not to fill the jobs.

Recent Trends

The help-wanted advertising index rose during the late 1970s, peaking at 157 in 1979. After declining to a low of 86 in 1982, it rose to 153 in 1987. Thus, while recovering most of the sharp decline in the early 1980s, the index in 1987 was still slightly below the 1979 level.

Reference from Primary Data Source

Noreen L. Preston, *The Help-wanted Index: Technical Description and Behavioral Trends*, The Conference Board, 1977.

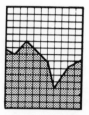

HOUSING STARTS

The housing starts indicator tracks the beginning of construction of new single family homes, townhouses, and multifamily apartment buildings. Each single family house and each separate apartment within apartment buildings (including cooperative and condominium buildings) is counted as one housing start. The measure includes privately owned and publicly owned housing but excludes placements of mobile homes, additions and alterations to existing housing, and conversions from nonresidential structures to residential use.

Where and When Available

Housing starts figures are provided by the Bureau of the Census in the U.S. Department of Commerce. The data are published in the report *Housing Starts*. Secondary sources include *Economic Indicators*, the *Survey of Current Business*, and the *Federal Reserve Bulletin*.

The data are available in a press release during the third week of the month after the month to which they refer. Each monthly report contains revised figures for the two previous months. The seasonally adjusted figures are revised every year for the preceding three years based on revised seasonal adjustment factors.

Content

Most housing starts are for privately owned housing. These are counted as occurring in the month that excavation work begins for the foundation. For publicly owned housing, however, the start is counted in the month that the construction contract is awarded to the prime contractor. This is done because these data are readily available and, due to the small volume of public housing, it is not considered cost effective to conduct a survey to determine when excavation work began. While each single family house and apartment unit is counted as one housing start, the effect of differences in size and amenities of each start with respect to the volume of construction work is only captured in figures on the dollar value of housing construction. (Other information is available on the number of housing units for which construction is completed every month, including size and amenities, in the report, *Characteristics of New Housing*.)

The housing starts figures are seasonally adjusted.

Methodology

Housing starts figures are estimated separately for privately owned housing in local areas that require building permits for construction, for private housing in nonpermit-issuing localities, and for publicly owned housing. For the permit-issuing areas, two monthly sample surveys are used: (1) a mail survey of 8,300 of the 17,000 permit-issuing localities to determine the total number of permits issued, and (2) a survey of 840 areas by on-site interviewers to determine in which month construction started on housing units which were authorized in previous months and the current month. The information obtained on-site about the rates of construction started for permits issued for each month to date is applied to the current permit figures to develop the total number of housing starts every month. The figures are adjusted upward to reflect starts begun in permit areas without a permit based on factors developed from surveys conducted in the late 1960s. The figures are also adjusted upwards to reflect units started before permit authorization and those for which late reports are received. These upward adjustments are based on factors derived from annual reviews of the extent to which these events occur.

Private housing starts in nonpermit areas are estimated from monthly on-site surveys of ongoing construction work in a sample of these localities. Data on public housing starts are obtained from the U.S. Department of Housing and Urban Development. Public housing constructed without federal aid is excluded, but it is very small.

Accuracy

The sampling error for housing starts in 2 cases out of 3 is plus or minus 3 percent and in 19 cases out of 20 is plus or minus 6 percent.

Relevance

New housing construction is important to the overall economy. Construction results in the hiring of workers, the production of construction materials and equipment, and the sale of large household appliances such as ranges and refrigerators. In addition, when owners or tenants occupy the housing, they often buy new furniture, carpeting, and other furnishings.

The rate of new housing construction is heavily influenced by the growth of the number of households in the long run and by the growth of real family income and the level of mortgage interest rates over shorter periods. Because housing lasts for many years and there is little need to replace it frequently, the purchase of new housing usually is deferred until incomes and interest rates make it affordable. Typically, housing starts increase when interest rates are low or incomes in general are rising, and they fall when interest rates are high or incomes are growing slowly or declining.

Housing starts fluctuate considerably during business cycles.

They are also classified as a leading indicator of business activity by the Bureau of Economic Analysis in the U.S. Department of Commerce. Housing permits are a component of the leading index of *leading, coincident, and lagging indexes*. The permit to construct a house is typically issued shortly before the beginning of construction, as reflected by the housing start—usually within three months in advance of the start of construction for single family homes, and within six months in advance for apartment buildings.

Recent Trends

After peaking in the late 1970s at 2.0 million units in 1977 and 1978, housing starts declined to 1.1 million in 1981 and 1982.

Table 25

Housing Starts
(thousands)

			Privately owned		
	Total	Total privately owned	Single family	Multi-family	Publicly owned
1975	1,171	1,160	892	268	11
1976	1,548	1,538	1,162	376	10
1977	2,002	1,987	1,451	536	15
1978	2,036	2,020	1,433	587	16
1979	1,760	1,745	1,194	551	15
1980	1,313	1,292	852	440	20
1981	1,100	1,084	705	379	16
1982	1,072	1,062	663	399	10
1983	1,713	1,703	1,068	635	9
1984	1,756	1,750	1,084	666	6
1985	1,745	1,742	1,072	670	3
1986	1,807	1,805	1,179	626	2
1987	1,623	1,621	1,146	474	2

Note: Detail may not add to totals due to rounding.

They subsequently rose to 1.8 million in 1986 and then declined to 1.6 million in 1987. Abstracting from these fluctuations, over the long run housing starts drifted downward from the late 1970s to the late 1980s.

The distribution of privately owned single family and multi-family housing starts changed over the 1975–87 period. Single family units declined steadily from 77 percent in 1975 to 62 percent in 1984 and 1985. The single family proportion then rose to 71 percent in 1987.

Publicly owned housing starts declined to negligible levels over this 13-year period. After peaking at 20,000 units in 1980, they declined to 2,000 units in 1986 and in 1987.

Reference from Primary Data Source

Bureau of the Census, U.S. Department of Commerce, *Housing Starts* (monthly).

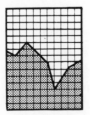

IMPORT AND EXPORT PRICE INDEXES

The import and export price indexes measure price changes in agricultural, mineral, and manufactured products for goods bought from and sold to foreigners. They represent increases and decreases in prices of internationally traded goods due to changes in the value of the dollar and changes in the markets for the items.

Where and When Available

Import and export price indexes are provided monthly and quarterly by the Bureau of Labor Statistics in the U.S. Department of Labor. The data are published in a press release and in the BLS monthly magazine, the *Monthly Labor Review*.

The figures are published at the end of the month immediately following the month or quarter to which they refer. They are revised in the following month or quarter. Major benchmark revisions, which include updating the weighting structure, are made approximately every five years. Smaller technical revisions such as introducing new products are made between benchmarks.

Content

The import and export price indexes cover most foreign traded goods. The broad product categories of the indexes are food; beverages and tobacco; crude materials; fuels; intermediate manufactured products; machinery and transportation equipment; and miscellaneous manufactured products. The quarterly figures cover approximately 22,000 products compared to the monthly coverage of 4,000 products. Military equipment, works of art, commercial aircraft and ships, and products with 1985 trade values below $500 million for exports and $700 million for imports are excluded.

(Supplementary price indexes are provided for a limited number of services entering the U.S.—electricity imported from Canada, air passenger fares on U.S. carriers, and crude oil tanker freight rates on tankers of all nationalities. These are not included in the above indexes for goods.)

Two sets of price indexes are provided for both imports and exports: one gauges price movements in terms of the dollar prices and the other in terms of foreign currency prices. The price movements in dollars show what Americans are paying for imports and receiving for exports. The price movements in foreign currency show what foreigners are receiving for exports to the United States (U.S. imports) and what they are paying for imports from the United States (U.S. exports). Differentials in the price movements of the dollar and foreign currency indexes reflect the extent to which changes in the value of the dollar are passed through to prices of the goods in U.S. and foreign markets.

For example, if the dollar declined 10 percent and, over the same period, export prices in foreign currencies rose 2 percent, U.S. exporters would have passed through 20 percent of the dollar decline in higher prices and absorbed 80 percent of the dollar decline in lower profit margins. Analogously, if a 10 percent decline in the dollar was accompanied by a 2 percent increase in import prices in dollars, foreign exporters passed through 20 percent of the dollar decline in higher prices and absorbed 80 percent of the decline in lower profit margins. These calculations are based on additional data provided with the price indexes that indicate the movement of the value of the dollar for each item weighted by the amount of trade with each country and the currency values of the foreign countries.

Prices represent the actual transaction value including premiums and discounts from list prices and changes in credit terms and packaging. The preferred price definition for imports is the value at the U.S. border including overseas transportation and insurance costs (c.i.f., cost-insurance-freight), but if c.i.f. values aren't readily available, then value at the foreign port of export (f.o.b., free-on-board) is used. For example, imports of food, beverages, and intermediate manufactured products are priced on a c.i.f. basis, and imports of machinery, transportation equipment, and miscellaneous manufactured products are priced on a f.o.b. basis. Import duties are excluded in both cases. The preferred price definition for exports is the value at the U.S. port of export before loading (f.a.s., free alongside ship), but if f.a.s. values are not readily available, the value f.o.b. at the U.S. factory or mine is used.

Prices usually are based on the time the item is delivered, not the time the order is placed. The indexes reflect movements for the same or similar item exclusive of enhancement or reduction in the quality or quantity of the item.

The import and export price indexes are not seasonally adjusted.

Methodology

The price data are obtained by a Bureau of Labor Statistics mail survey from a sample of over 8,300 importers and exporters for the quarterly indexes and over 1,900 importers and exporters for the monthly indexes, including a limited number of foreign trade brokers. The overall response rate to the BLS survey is 90 percent. In addition, prices of crude petroleum imports are based on U.S. Department of Energy data and those for grain exports, excluding rice, are based on U.S. Department of Agriculture data. Price quotations are sought for the first transactions of the third month of the quarter for the quarterly figures (March, June, September, and December), typically within the first two weeks of the month; if there are no transactions in that period, either the previous or subsequent two-week period is used.

Since 1988, the weights of the indexes for 1985 and subsequent years have been based on the 1985 dollar value of imports or exports for each item as reported by the Census Bureau. The weights were based on the 1980 value of foreign trade prior to 1985.

If the reported import or export price includes a change in the quality or quantity of the item, an adjustment is made to compensate for the improvement or decline in order to measure price movements for items having the same functional characteristics over time. Because data to make the necessary adjustments are not always available, the import and export price indexes contain an unknown amount of price change caused by quality and quantity changes. (See the *consumer price index* and *producer price indexes* for examples.)

Accuracy

There are no estimates of sampling or revision error for the import and export price indexes.

Relevance

The import and export price indexes help to gauge changes in the competitive position of U.S. imports and exports and to analyze the effect of this changing competitive position on the volume of import and export trade. The price indexes are useful in evaluating the effect of changes in the value of the dollar on import and export prices. This information also makes it possible to perform a limited analysis of the effect of changes in the dollar on U.S. domestic price *inflation*.

Recent Trends

Import prices measured in dollars (to U.S. buyers) increased substantially for all goods in 1987, following decreases or only slight increases from 1983 to 1986. However, because of the decline in the dollar beginning in March 1985, import prices measured in foreign currency (to foreign sellers) declined noticeably in 1986 and 1987. Part of the softness in import prices from 1983 to 1986, and especially in 1986, reflected the international decline in oil prices. Export prices in dollar terms increased in 1987, following three years of successive decline. However, measured in foreign currency, American exporters charged lower prices in 1986 and 1987 because the decline in the dollar more than offset the higher prices.

Table 26

**Import and Export Price Indexes
(annual percent change)**

	All imports		Imports excluding fuels		All exports	
	Dollar price	Foreign currency price	Dollar price	Foreign currency price	Dollar price	Foreign currency price
December to December						
1983	−2.5%	NA	2.1%	NA	NA	NA
1984	−1.7	NA	−1.0	NA	−1.4	NA
1985	0.8	NA	2.1	NA	−0.9	NA
1986	0.3	−9.4	8.2	−3.6	−0.7	−8.8
1987	10.2	−4.7	9.1	−6.2	6.0	−6.9

NA = Not available

References from Primary Data Source

Bureau of Labor Statistics, U.S. Department of Labor, *BLS Handbook of Methods*, April 1988, Chapter 17.

"BLS Announces New Price Data for Imports and Exports," Press Release, November 18, 1987.

William Alterman, David S. Johnson, and John Goth, "BLS publishes average exchange rate and foreign currency price indexes," *Monthly Labor Review*, December 1987.

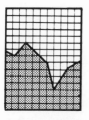

INDUSTRIAL PRODUCTION INDEX

The industrial production index (IPI) measures the change in output in U.S. manufacturing, mining, and electric and gas utilities industries. Output refers to the physical quantity of items produced, as distinct from sales value which combines quantity and price. The index covers the production of goods and power for domestic sales in the United States and exports. It excludes production in the agriculture, construction, transportation, communication, trade, finance, and service industries; government output; and imports. While the excluded industries and imports are not directly in the IPI, they are indirectly incorporated to the extent that the manufacturing, mining, and utilities industries use them as intermediate items, in which case they are a component of the product or power produced.

Where and When Available

The IPI is prepared monthly by the Federal Reserve Board. It is published in a press release and in the *Federal Reserve Bulletin*, the FRB's monthly magazine. Secondary sources include *Economic Indicators*, the *Survey of Current Business*, and *Business Conditions Digest*.

The figures are available in the middle of the month after the month to which they refer. Preliminary data are provided for the preceding month; these are revised in the subsequent three months. Annual revisions are made in the fall.

Content

The IPI is provided from two perspectives: (1) output originating in the producing industries (supply) and (2) selected consumer and business markets of the items produced (demand). The component groups of the supply perspective are the producing industries: manufacturing, mining, and electric and gas utilities. For the market perspective, these components are categorized as products according to their typical usage. These are: consumer goods, business equipment, defense and space equipment, intermediate products including construction and business supplies, and materials including parts, containers, and raw materials.

The official monthly index is based on the total in the market grouping because of the greater interest in the cyclical aspects of the economy associated with changes in demand. The two alternative totals typically differ by no more than 0.1 percentage point from month to month.

The IPI is currently based on 1977 = 100.

The IPI figures are seasonally adjusted.

Methodology

The IPI is developed by weighting each component according to its relative importance in the base period. (See the section on index numbers in the Introduction.) The information for weights is obtained from the value added measures of production in the economic censuses of manufacturers and minerals industries and from value added information for the utility industries in Internal Revenue Service statistics of income data. Value added generally refers to the wages, profits, and depreciation of capital facilities in the producing industry, i.e., the value an industry adds to goods and services it buys from other industries, although there are technical differences in the definition of value added as it is used in the economic censuses and the *gross national product*. The weights are updated at five-year intervals that coincide with the economic censuses. The monthly movements of the index are based on the following information: production of actual items (43 percent); electric kilowatt hour consumption by producing industries (30 percent); production worker hours in producing industries (25 percent); and a combination of electric consumption with worker hours plus miscellaneous sources (2 percent).

In the annual revisions, monthly movements of the IPI components which were estimated from indirect sources (kilowatt hours and worker hours) are corrected to reflect more extensive direct data on production, which is obtained mainly from the Census Bureau's annual survey of manufacturers.

Accuracy

Revisions to the IPI preliminary monthly levels and to the monthly movements are usually within a range of plus or minus 0.3 percent.

Relevance

The coverage of the IPI makes it a sensitive gauge of the most cyclical aspects of the economy. Although the industries covered amounted to only 25 percent of the GNP in 1986, they account for the bulk of the more volatile movements in expansions and recessions. Consequently, the IPI tends to rise more in expansions and fall more in recessions than the overall economy. The IPI is a component of the coincident index of the *leading, coincident, and lagging indexes*.

For short-run cyclical analysis, the market categories are of particular interest. They are helpful in assessing the effect of changes in demand on industrial output. For longer-run analysis, the IPI industrial categories are more significant. These industries are important customers of the noncovered industries such as agriculture, transportation, communication, and services and, thus, have a significant secondary effect on the growth of the rest of the economy. Generally, the overall economy does not grow rapidly unless the IPI expands even more robustly.

Table 27

Industrial Production Index
(1977 = 100)

		Market Categories			
	Total	Consumer goods	Equipment	Intermediate products	Materials
1975	84.8	84.9	88.5	83.6	83.2
1976	92.6	93.3	91.5	92.1	93.0
1977	100.0	100.0	100.0	100.0	100.0
1978	106.5	104.3	110.3	106.9	105.9
1979	110.7	103.9	120.4	110.8	110.3
1980	108.6	102.7	124.7	106.9	105.3
1981	111.0	104.1	129.9	107.3	107.7
1982	103.1	101.4	120.2	101.7	96.7
1983	109.2	109.3	121.7	111.2	102.8
1984	121.4	118.0	139.6	124.7	114.2
1985	123.7	119.8	145.8	129.3	114.3
1986	125.1	124.0	143.6	136.2	113.8
1987	129.8	127.8	148.9	143.4	118.2

			Industry Categories		
	Total	Percent change	Manufacturing	Mining	Utilities
1975	84.8	−8.8%	83.4	96.6	93.7
1976	92.6	9.2	91.9	97.4	97.4
1977	100.0	8.0	100.0	100.0	100.0
1978	106.5	6.5	107.1	103.6	103.1
1979	110.7	3.9	111.5	106.4	105.9
1980	108.6	−1.9	108.2	112.4	107.3
1981	111.0	2.2	110.5	117.5	107.1
1982	103.1	−7.1	102.2	109.3	104.8
1983	109.2	5.9	110.2	102.9	105.2
1984	121.4	11.2	123.4	111.1	110.7
1985	123.7	1.9	126.4	108.9	111.1
1986	125.1	1.1	129.1	100.4	108.5
1987	129.8	3.6	134.7	100.7	110.3

Recent Trends

The IPI rose rapidly in the late 1970s, although at a declining rate of increase, slowing from a 9 percent increase in 1976 to 4 percent in 1979. There was no overall growth in the IPI from 1979 to 1983 and declines occurred in 1980 and 1982. Following a sharp increase in 1984, annual increases during 1985-87 were 1 to 3.5 percent.

There were marked variations in growth among the market and industry components over the 1975-87 period. Equipment and intermediate products showed the most rapid increases while consumer goods and materials had the slowest. Manufacturing increased much faster than utilities and mining (in 1986 and 1987, mining was at the 1977 level).

References from Primary Data Source

Board of Governors of the Federal Reserve System, *Industrial Production 1986 Edition: With a Description of the Methodology*, 1986.

Joan D. Hosley and James E. Kennedy, "A Revision of the Index of Industrial Production," *Federal Reserve Bulletin*, July 1985.

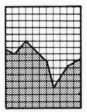

INFLATION

Inflation is a rise in the general level of prices. A decline in overall prices, which occurs less frequently, is known as deflation. Six measures of inflation are covered in this book: the *consumer price index, CRB futures price index, farm parity ratio, GNP price measures, import and export price indexes,* and *producer price indexes*.

Because the prices of particular items of goods and services, such as food, housing, transportation, clothing, medical care, energy, equipment, containers, lumber, chemicals, and metals, rise and fall at different rates, price measures that include different items and combine the items in different ways show different overall rates of price change. Since the six price measures cover different items and are constructed using different methodologies, they show different rates of price change.

In addition, prices of food and energy are highly volatile due to the effect of unpredictable weather conditions on crop harvests and the uncertainty of the Organization of Petroleum Exporting Countries as an effective cartel in managing oil production and prices. In the 1970s and 1980s, prices of food and energy generally diverged noticeably from other items, with food and energy showing higher price increases during the 1970s and lower increases in the 1980s. Because food and energy prices are linked to vagaries like the weather and OPEC, economists developed a concept called the "underlying rate of inflation," which refers to price movements of goods and services except for food and energy. These measures are regularly published for the consumer price index and the producer price indexes.

Various terms are used to distinguish differing rates of price change. Overall, price increases are referred to as inflation and price decreases are called deflation. More specifically, price increases below 2 percent annually are known as "creeping inflation"; price increases that become progressively larger each year are "accelerating inflation"; price increases either approaching or above 10 percent annually are "hyperinflation"; a reduction in the rate of inflation is "disinflation"; and no change in the annual price level is "zero inflation."

Inflation affects the purchasing power of peoples' income and wealth (*personal income and saving*); the ability to manage the economy through fiscal and monetary policies (*government budgets and debt, money supply, interest rates*); the tendency to channel funds into different types of investment (*plant and equipment expenditures, housing starts, stock market prices and dividend yields*); and our ability to compete in world markets (*balance of trade, balance of payments, value of the dollar*). A low rate of inflation is a basic goal of economic policy because it protects purchasing power; helps in designing fiscal and monetary policies to promote economic growth; encourages investment in the production of goods and services as distinct from speculation in stocks, real estate, art work, and gambling; and makes U.S. goods more competitive at home and abroad. Inflation sometimes moves inversely to *unemployment*, where an increase in inflation is accompanied by a decrease in unemployment and an increase in inflation is accompanied by a decrease in unemployment. When this adverse tradeoff occurs, the goal of lower inflation may be relaxed in favor of lower unemployment, as provided for in the Full Employment and Balanced Growth Act of 1978 (Humphrey-Hawkins Act).

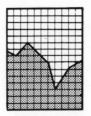

INTEREST RATES

Interest represents the cost of borrowing money. An interest rate, also referred to as a yield, is the annualized percent that interest is of the principal of the loan. The level of interest rates for different loans reflects the length and risk of the loan. Generally, short-term loans have lower interest rates than long-term loans, and loans subject to little risk of not being repaid have lower interest rates than those with higher risk. The main exception occurs during periods of high *inflation* when the Federal Reserve Board tightens bank credit to lower the inflation rate, which temporarily drives short-term interest rates above long-term rates.

Where and When Available

Measures of interest rates for different types of loans are provided variously on a daily, weekly, or monthly basis by the Federal Reserve Board, Federal Reserve Bank of New York, Federal Home Loan Bank Board, Moody's Investors Service, Standard & Poor's Corporation, and American Banker-Bond Buyer. They are published in press releases, the *Federal Reserve Bulletin*, *Moody's Bond Survey*, Standard & Poor's *Outlook*, and the American Banker-Bond Buyer *Bond Buyer Index*. Secondary sources include *Economic Indicators*, the *Survey of Current Business*, and *Business Conditions Digest*.

The figures are available within a day to a week after the period to which they refer. Some of the measures are revised for the previous month.

Content

The nine interest rate measures covered here show the different costs of borrowing for short-term, medium-term, and long-term loans of high quality. Loans of high quality have the least risk of nonpayment. While all of these nine types are high quality loans, some are more secure than others—for example, U.S. Treasury securities are default free and, thus, are the highest quality. Loan periods may be broadly defined as up to one year (short-term), one to three years (medium-term), and more than three years (long-term). Some interest rates are for new loans, while others are for outstanding loans that are traded in securities markets. The loans are made to federal, state, and local governments; households; nonbank industries; and commercial banks.

Depending on the type of loan instrument, interest rates are measured according to one of three methods: (1) paying a certain amount at regularly specified intervals with a bond coupon or through negotiated terms of the loan, (2) the extent to which the par value (redemption price when the security expires) of a non-coupon security is above the discounted market price of the security, or (3) a hybrid of regular interest and a premium or discounted market price from the par value of the security.

Interest rate figures are not seasonally adjusted.

The nine kinds of interest rates are summarized below. Sources of the interest rate figures are in parenthesis.

U.S. TREASURY THREE-MONTH BILLS (U.S. Treasury): Short-term default-free borrowing of new issues sold at a discount from the par value.

U.S. TREASURY NOTES AND BONDS WITH AVERAGE CONSTANT MATURITIES OF THREE AND TEN YEARS (Federal Reserve Board): Medium-term and long-term default-free outstanding issues sold with a coupon interest rate and at a premium or discount from the par value. These are averages of securities that encompass a range of maturities from under three years to over ten years and, thus, do not focus on a particular issue.

HIGH-GRADE MUNICIPAL BONDS (Standard & Poor's): Long-term outstanding issues of state and local governments sold with a coupon interest rate and at a premium or discount from the par value. They are exempt from federal taxes.

BOND BUYER INDEX FOR MUNICIPAL BONDS (American Banker-Bond Buyer): Theoretical yields for long-term new issues of state and local governments representing a hypothetical new issue sold at par value. They are not actual yields, but representative of what yields would be if issues were offered on the market. The bonds would be exempt from federal taxes.

CORPORATE AAA BONDS (Moody's Investors Service): Long-term industrial and public utility outstanding issues sold with a coupon interest rate and at a premium or discount from the par value.

PRIME COMMERCIAL PAPER (Federal Reserve Bank of New York): Short-term borrowing by large companies sold at a discount from the par value.

FEDERAL RESERVE DISCOUNT RATE (Federal Reserve Bank of New York): Short-term borrowing by commercial banks from regional Federal Reserve banks to meet seasonal demands for money, to maintain certain reserve levels over a two-week period, to meet huge outflows at the end of a day, or to keep bank reserves from falling close to or below legal minimum requirements.

PRIME RATE CHARGED BY COMMERCIAL BANKS (Federal Reserve Board): Threshold interest rate for short-term business loans, with loans to small companies above the prime rate and loans to large companies below the prime rate.

NEW HOME MORTGAGE YIELDS (Federal Home Loan Bank Board): The "effective rate" at closings of conventional first mortgage loans for fixed and variable rate mortgages for newly built, single family, nonfarm homes amortized over ten years. This rate includes the contract interest rate and points, as well as certain other costs such as realtor commissions, credit and appraisal reports, and attorneys' fees. The ten-year amortization period is a rough approximation of the average life of a conventional mortgage.

(The Federal Home Loan Mortgage Corporation provides a weekly home mortgage rate based on mortgage commitments (prospective interest rates) for new and existing single family homes. This differs from the above FHLBB rate which represents closings (actual interest rates) for new homes on a monthly basis. The FHLMC rate is noted here to acquaint the reader with an indicator of future mortgage interest rates.)

Methodology

The bonds, loans, and commercial paper for particular companies and governments that are used in calculating the interest rate measures are changed from time to time. They are replaced with others, as needed, in order to maintain the measure's criteria for the length of maturity and quality of the loans and to prevent extraordinary price movements in a single security from distorting the total measure.

U.S. TREASURY THREE-MONTH BILLS: The discounted price of the auction conducted every Tuesday is the weekly yield. These weekly yields are averaged to obtain the monthly figure.

U.S. TREASURY NOTES AND BONDS WITH AVERAGE CONSTANT MATURITIES OF THREE AND TEN YEARS: Yield curves are constructed by plotting interest rates on the vertical axis of a graph and years to maturity on the horizontal axis. A line is drawn through the middle of the plotted points and the interest rate is read from the line that corresponds to three and ten years. The daily closing yields are averaged to obtain the weekly figure, and the weekly figures are averaged for the monthly yield.

HIGH-GRADE MUNICIPAL BONDS: The yields of general obligation issues for 15 states and localities with a maturity of approximately twenty years are averaged arithmetically using equal weights for each issue. The Wednesday closing bid quotation is used as the weekly yield, and the weekly figures are averaged for the monthly yield.

BOND BUYER INDEX FOR MUNICIPAL BONDS: Municipal bond dealers and banks are surveyed each week for their opinions on what a hypothetical new coupon bond for 11 states and localities would yield if the issue sold at par value. The 11 yields are averaged arithmetically using equal weights.

CORPORATE AAA BONDS: Yields for samples of less than ten industrial issues and of ten public utility issues with maturities of more than fifteen years are averaged arithmetically using equal weights in two steps: (1) separate averages are calculated for the industrial and public utility groups, and (2) the two group figures are averaged into a single figure. Daily closing prices (or the average of the closing bid and asked price) are averaged to obtain the weekly and monthly figures.

PRIME COMMERCIAL PAPER: Based on surveys of New York City dealers, daily quotation prices of issues with six-month maturities (four to six months before 1980) are averaged arithmetically with equal weights for the weekly and monthly figures.

FEDERAL RESERVE DISCOUNT RATE: These rates of the 12 regional Federal Reserve banks must be approved by the Federal Reserve Board. The rates of all 12 regional banks are the same, except for periods of a day or two when changes are not made simultaneously. Officially, the rate for the Federal Reserve Bank of New York is used, but, in practice, the New York rate is the same as those of the other regional banks.

PRIME RATE CHARGED BY BANKS: The daily rates charged by a majority of 29 large money market banks (referred to as the "predominant rate") are averaged to obtain the weekly and monthly figures.

NEW HOME MORTGAGE YIELDS: A sample of savings and loan associations, commercial banks, mutual savings banks, and mortgage bankers are surveyed for yields on mortgage loans for newly built, single family homes. The survey covers mortgage closings during the first five working days of the month. Interest rates of the various lenders are weighted by the share of the mortgage holdings of each type of lender and averaged arithmetically.

Accuracy

There are no estimates of sampling or revision error for the interest rate figures.

Relevance

Interest rates have a significant impact on borrowing and spending. Generally, household, business, and government borrowings are stimulated when interest rates are perceived as low and are restrained when interest rates are perceived as high. The "low" and "high" designations are based on borrowers' assessments of past levels and prospective movements. If interest rates are expected to rise, there is an incentive to borrow immediately, but if interest rates are expected to fall, there is an incentive to delay borrowing. Interest rates react to and influence movements of the *gross national product, money supply, inflation*, and *value of the dollar*.

Table 28

Interest Rates
(percent)

	U.S. Treasury 3-month bills	Discount rate: Federal Reserve Bank of New York	Prime commercial paper	Prime rate charged by banks	Bond buyer index (11 bonds)
1975	5.84%	6.25%	6.32%	7.86%	6.61%
1976	4.99	5.50	5.34	6.84	6.11
1977	5.27	5.46	5.61	6.83	5.38
1978	7.22	7.46	7.99	9.06	5.72
1979	10.04	10.28	10.91	12.67	6.18
1980	11.51	11.77	12.29	15.27	8.15
1981	14.03	13.41	14.76	18.87	10.98
1982	10.69	11.02	11.89	14.86	11.26
1983	8.63	8.50	8.89	10.79	9.26
1984	9.58	8.80	10.16	12.04	9.98
1985	7.48	7.69	8.01	9.93	9.01
1986	5.98	6.33	6.39	8.33	7.21
1987	5.82	5.66	6.85	8.22	7.53

	High-grade municipal bonds	U.S. Treasury 3-year constant maturities	U.S. Treasury 10-year constant maturities	Corporate AAA bonds	New home mortgage yields
1975	6.89%	7.49%	7.99%	8.83%	9.00%
1976	6.49	6.77	7.61	8.43	9.00
1977	5.56	6.69	7.42	8.02	9.02
1978	5.90	8.29	8.41	8.73	9.56
1979	6.39	9.71	9.44	9.63	10.78
1980	8.51	11.55	11.46	11.94	12.66
1981	11.23	14.44	13.91	14.17	14.70
1982	11.57	12.92	13.00	13.79	15.14
1983	9.47	10.45	11.10	12.04	12.57
1984	10.15	11.89	12.44	12.71	12.38
1985	9.18	9.64	10.62	11.37	11.55
1986	7.38	7.06	7.68	9.02	10.17
1987	7.73	7.68	8.39	9.38	9.31

Recent Trends

In general, virtually all interest rates rose from the late 1970s through 1981, subsequently declined through 1986, and rose slightly in 1987. Among the loan categories, short-term loans (Treasury three-month bills, commercial paper, the prime rate, and the Federal Reserve discount rate) typically have lower interest rates than medium- and long-term loans (Treasury three- and ten-year constant maturities, state and local bonds, corporate bonds, and new home mortgages). The major exception to this pattern occurred during the high inflation of 1979–81, when short-term rates were higher than long-term rates. Within the short-term group, the lowest rates typically are the discount rate and those for three-month bills, followed by commercial paper and the prime rate. Within the medium- and long-term group, the lowest rates are those for the tax-exempt state and local bonds and Treasury three-year bonds, followed by Treasury ten-year bonds, corporate bonds, and new home mortgages.

References from Primary Data Sources

Board of Governors of the Federal Reserve System, *Annual Statistical Digest*.

Arthur W. Samansky, *Statfacts: Understanding Federal Reserve Statistical Reports*, Federal Reserve Bank of New York, November 1981.

Federal Home Loan Bank Board, "Interest Rates and Other Characteristics of Conventional First Mortgage Loans Originated on Single Family Homes: Data Users Guide," May 1986 (unpublished).

American Banker-Bond Buyer, *1988 Bond Buyer Index*.

Moody's Investors Service, *Moody's Bond Survey* (weekly), *Moody's Bond Record* (monthly), and "Moody's Bond Yield Averages—Description of Averages and Method of Computation" (unpublished), continuously updated.

Standard and Poor's Corporation, Statistical Service, *Security Price Index Record*, 1988 edition.

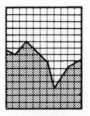

INTERNATIONAL INVESTMENT POSITION OF THE UNITED STATES

The U.S. international investment position represents the cumulative value of U.S. assets abroad and of foreign assets in the United States. It is commonly referred to as the overall creditor or debtor status of the nation, although technically it only partially represents debt because it also includes equity ownership of foreign companies. Nevertheless, in this discussion, the creditor and debtor designations will be used because they reflect the general perception of the meaning of the figures. If American assets abroad exceed foreign assets in the U.S., the United States is a creditor nation, and if foreign assets in the U.S. exceed American assets abroad, the U.S. is a debtor nation. International assets include production facilities, bonds, stocks, loans, official U.S. reserves of gold, the U.S. reserve position and special drawing rights in the International Monetary Fund, and U.S. holdings of foreign currencies.

Where and When Available

The Bureau of Economic Analysis in the U.S. Department of Commerce provides annual measures of the U.S. international investment position. They are published in a press release and in BEA's monthly magazine, the *Survey of Current Business*. Secondary sources include the *Economic Report of the President*.

The figures are available every June for the preceding year;

they are revised in the succeeding years as part of the annual *balance of payments* revisions. The annual revisions also change the figures for several of the preceding years.

Content

The net investment position of the United States is defined as assets abroad minus foreign assets in the U.S. The items included in assessing this investment position are the official, government, and private asset and liability components of the *balance of payments*. (U.S. assets abroad are "assets" and foreign assets in the United States are "liabilities.") The net investment position reflects the total U.S. and foreign assets outstanding at the end of each year, while the figures in the balance of payments reflect the annual increase or decrease in assets. The investment position figures include both the actual capital flows of these items in the balance of payments plus valuation changes. Geographic detail is provided for the countries of Canada and Japan, and the regions of Western Europe, Latin America, and other western hemisphere areas, other countries, plus international organizations.

The annual change in the investment position is attributable to four separately identified factors: (1) capital flows of the official, government, and private assets; (2) changes in the prices of bond and stock securities; (3) the effect of foreign exchange rate changes on the value of securities and on the U.S. official reserve; and (4) other changes associated with methodology, such as one-time changes in the item and respondent coverage in statistical surveys or one-time changes in the valuation of assets. Methodological changes result in a break in the comparability of the data series.

Methodology

The main data sources used in developing the investment position indicator are: Treasury Department surveys conducted by the

Federal Reserve Bank of New York on international assets and
liabilities; BEA surveys of foreign direct investment abroad and
in the United States; and the *value of the dollar* based on Federal
Reserve Board and Treasury Department measures. Breakdowns
of the factors contributing to the changes in position from year to
year are also derived from these data.

Direct investments (when 10 percent or more of the asset
is owned by the foreign investor) are measured in terms of
the book value of the company, while investments in securities and currency are measured in terms of their current market
value.

Accuracy

There are no estimates of sampling or revision error in the investment position figures. Increases and decreases in the position
from year to year attributable to methodological changes in the
data sources ("other changes") indicate the net effect of inconsistencies in the various data sources. (This is an overall minimum
assessment of the inconsistencies because offsetting errors
among the data elements reduce the net effect.) Because much of
the U.S. direct investment abroad was made in earlier years while
a greater proportion of foreign direct investment in the U.S.
occurred in recent years, the use of book value figures tends to
understate the amount of U.S. investment abroad relative to foreign investment in the United States. The valuation of the official
gold holdings at $42.22 per ounce also understates their value,
because the current market price is over $400 per ounce. Both of
these factors result in understating the U.S. creditor position or
overstating the U.S. debtor position. By contrast, the "statistical
discrepancy" in the *balance of payments* has shown a net inflow
of unrecorded funds into the U.S. since the mid-1970s. If the
unrecorded inflows are capital funds, foreign assets in the U.S.
would be understated. For all of these reasons, the international
investment position is an order of magnitude rather than a precise
figure.

Relevance

The international investment position reflects the international industrial and financial base of the United States. A creditor status signifies that Americans own more capital abroad than foreigners own in the U.S., while a debtor status indicates that Americans own less capital abroad than foreigners own in the U.S. Because a creditor nation is less dependent on outside sources of financing than a debtor nation, its capital funding requirements are less vulnerable to changes in international financial markets. Therefore, a creditor nation is more independent than a debtor nation in conducting monetary policies to manage its economy with respect to the economic effects of *interest rates* at home and abroad and the *value of the dollar*.

A creditor nation has a net inflow and a debtor nation has a net outflow of interest and dividend incomes paid on international loans and investments. If a nation is creditor, the income flows increase exports, which results in a surplus (or reduction in the deficit) in its *balance of payments*; if the nation is a debtor, the income flows increase imports, which results in a deficit (or reduction in the surplus) in its *balance of payments*. The income flows also tend to raise the wealth and standard of living in creditor nations relative to debtor nations. However, creditor nations risk adverse actions by debtor nations—default on foreign debt and expropriation of foreign-owned properties.

Recent Trends

There was a major shift in the U.S. creditor/deficit status over the 1975–87 period. Prior to 1985, the United States had been a creditor nation since 1915. The U.S. creditor position peaked at $141 billion in 1981, almost twice the 1975 level of $74 billion. During the 1982–87 period, the creditor status changed sharply and continuously to a debtor position of $368 billion in 1987. The shift reflected a marked slowdown in the rate of increase in U.S. assets abroad during the 1981–87 period compared to the

1975–81 period. Foreign assets in the United States rose at similar rates in both the earlier and later periods.

Table 29

International Investment Position of the U.S.
(billions of dollars)

Yearend	Net investment position	U.S. assets abroad	Foreign assets in the U.S.
1975	74.2	295.1	220.9
1976	83.6	347.2	263.6
1977	72.7	379.1	306.4
1978	76.1	447.8	371.7
1979	94.5	510.6	416.1
1980	106.3	607.1	500.8
1981	141.1	719.8	578.7
1982	136.9	824.9	688.1
1983	89.4	873.9	784.5
1984	3.5	896.1	892.6
1985	−110.7	950.3	1,061.0
1986	−269.2	1,071.4	1,340.7
1987	−368.2	1,167.8	1,536.0

Reference from Primary Data Source

Russell B. Scholl, "The International Investment Position of the United States in 1987," *Survey of Current Business*, June 1988. (This annual article is published every June.)

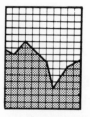

INVENTORY-SALES RATIOS

The inventory-sales ratio, in which inventories are in the numerator and sales in the denominator, represents the monthly turnover of inventories at current sales rates. For example, a ratio of 1.6 means that existing inventories will be used up in 1.6 months if sales continue at the current rate (assuming that inventories aren't replenished during the period).

Two basic measures of inventory-sales ratios are published. They differ in the definition of sales and in industry coverage. One is provided by the Bureau of the Census and the other is provided by the Bureau of Economic Analysis.

Where and When Available

BUREAU OF THE CENSUS. The Census Bureau in the U.S. Department of Commerce publishes monthly inventory-sales ratios in a press release. Secondary sources include *Economic Indicators* and the *Survey of Current Business*.

The figures are available 45 days after the month to which they refer; they are revised in the next month. Annual revisions are made in the spring of the following year, and comprehensive benchmark revisions are made about every five years.

BUREAU OF ECONOMIC ANALYSIS. The BEA in the U.S. Department of Commerce provides quarterly inventory-sales ratios as part of the *gross national product*. The measures are published in the *Survey of Current Business*.

The figures are available during the third or fourth week of the month after the quarter to which they refer (April for the first quarter, July for the second quarter, etc.); they are revised in the subsequent two months. More detailed revisions are made annually every July, and comprehensive benchmark revisions are made about every five years.

Content

BUREAU OF THE CENSUS. The Census Bureau's inventory-sales ratios reflect inventories and sales of manufacturers, merchant wholesalers, and retailers. They include sales of raw materials, supplies, and semi-finished goods to other businesses that reprocess them for later sale; sales of finished goods by manufacturers to wholesalers and retailers who resell them in the same state; and sales of finished goods to ultimate users. The inventory-sales ratios are provided in current dollars.

The inventory-sales ratios are seasonally adjusted.

BUREAU OF ECONOMIC ANALYSIS. The BEA's inventory-final sales ratios are confined to final sales to consumers, businesses, governments, and foreigners and, thus, exclude sales of raw materials, supplies, and semi-finished goods that are used up as intermediate products in the production process. They also exclude sales of finished goods from manufacturers to wholesalers and retailers who resell them in the same state. The inventory-final sales ratios are provided in current and constant dollars. (Inventory-sales ratios, as distinct from inventory-final sales ratios, are provided for manufacturing and trade industries in constant dollars.)

The final sales measures include agriculture, mining, construction, transportation, utilities, and services, as well as manufacturing and wholesale and retail trade. Final sales exclude gross products of households and institutions, governments, and the rest of the world (gross product refers to the income side of the *gross national product*).

The inventory-final sales ratios are seasonally adjusted.

Methodology

BUREAU OF THE CENSUS. The inventory and sales data are obtained from Census Bureau monthly surveys of manufacturers, merchant wholesalers, and retailers. The inventory figures are defined at current cost valuation, which is the book value acquisition cost before the companies convert inventories to a LIFO (last-in, first-out) valuation.

BUREAU OF ECONOMIC ANALYSIS. The inventory data for manufacturing and trade are based on the above noted Census Bureau surveys. The BEA adjusts these inventory data to put them on a replacement cost basis. That is, the inventories' current book value is based on prices when the inventories were acquired; BEA revalues them to reflect prices in the current period. BEA also adjusts the inventory data for other industries to reflect replacement cost. The inventory figures for these other industries are obtained from the U.S. Department of Agriculture, the U.S. Department of Energy, and the Internal Revenue Service. The IRS annual figures are the main source for the inventory levels of these other industries. These data are in turn extrapolated to the current quarter based on current data, such as is available for petroleum bulk stations and electric utilities, or by recent annual trends.

Final sales are based on the final sales figures in the *gross national product*, excluding gross product of households and institutions, governments, and the rest of the world. The constant dollar figures are based mainly on price changes in the *producer price indexes*.

Accuracy

BUREAU OF THE CENSUS. There are no estimates of sampling or revision error for the inventory-sales ratios for the combined total of manufacturing and trade industries. Estimates of sampling error are available for the wholesale and retail trade components separately.

BUREAU OF ECONOMIC ANALYSIS. There are no estimates of sampling or revision error for the inventory-final sales figures.

Relevance

Inventory-sales ratios have significant implications for future production levels. Inventories are a business cost. Businesses finance inventories by borrowing funds or tying up their own money. Thus, high inventory-sales ratios suggest that businesses will tend to cut back on orders to suppliers because it is expensive to hold goods that are not selling rapidly. The resulting lower *manufacturers' orders* lead to lower production and employment levels. Analogously, low inventory-sales ratios suggest increased orders to replenish inventories, because the ability to furnish items readily off-the-shelf and maintaining a wider selection of goods for customers will promote sales. In this case, the growth in orders results in higher production and employment.

These general tendencies hold true, more or less, depending on the extent to which inventory movements result from deliberate action by businesses to build up or deplete inventories through sales incentives, cost cutting, changes in production and orders (planned inventory change), or from unanticipated inventory accumulations or depletions due to shifts in customer demand (unplanned inventory change). Unplanned inventory changes may affect future production more because of the surprise effect they have on business expectations. Unanticipated changes are not quantifiable because the inventory data do not distinguish the planned and unplanned components. The inventory-sales ratio in constant dollars is a component of the lagging index of the *leading, coincident, and lagging indexes*.

Recent Trends

BUREAU OF THE CENSUS. The inventory-sales ratio for manufacturing and trade industries fluctuated within a range of 1.45 to 1.52 over the 1975–87 period, with the major exception being 1.67 in 1982. There was no upward or downward trend over the 12-year period.

BUREAU OF ECONOMIC ANALYSIS. The inventory-final sales ratio for nonfarm industries in both current and constant dollars drifted downward over the 1975–87 period. The current dollar figures declined from peak levels of 3.25 in the late 1970s to 2.7 in the mid-1980s. The constant dollar figures declined from 3.1 in the same time periods.

Table 30

**Selected Inventory-Sales Ratios
(months)**

	Ratio for total sales: manufacturing and trade (current dollars) December	Ratio for final sales: nonfarm industries (current dollars) 4th quarter	Ratio for final sales: nonfarm industries (constant dollars) 4th quarter
1975	1.52	3.11	3.08
1976	1.47	3.14	3.09
1977	1.45	3.10	3.10
1978	1.44	3.12	3.08
1979	1.44	3.24	3.08
1980	1.41	3.26	3.07
1981	1.52	3.25	3.16
1982	1.67	3.02	3.04
1983	1.48	2.87	2.92
1984	1.54	2.89	3.00
1985	1.52	2.73	2.90
1986	1.47	2.61	2.89
1987	1.52	2.68	2.93

References from Primary Data Sources

Bureau of the Census, U.S. Department of Commerce, *Manufacturing and Trade Inventories and Sales*, monthly. More detailed Census Bureau descriptions of the methodology are in *Manufacturers' Shipments, Inventories, and Orders*, annual; *Wholesale Trade*, annual; and *Retail Trade*, annual.

Carol S. Carson, "GNP: An Overview of Source Data and Estimating Methods," *Survey of Current Business*, July 1987.

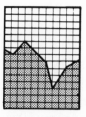

LEADING, COINCIDENT, AND LAGGING INDEXES

The leading, coincident, and lagging (LCLg) indexes are an analytic system for assessing current and future economic trends, particularly cyclical expansions and recessions. The system is based on grouping some key indicators according to their tendency to change direction before, during, or after the general economy turns from a recession to an expansion or from an expansion to a recession. Indicators in the leading index change direction before a cyclical turning point in the general economy; those in the coincident index change direction at the same time; and those in the lagging index change direction after the general economy. In substance, the leading index reflects business commitments and expectations, the coincident index reflects the current pace of the economy, and the lagging index reflects business costs. The three indexes are called composite indexes because they group several component indicators.

Where and When Available

The Bureau of Economic Analysis in the U.S. Department of Commerce provides monthly measures of the LCLg indexes. They are published in a press release and in BEA's monthly magazines, *Business Conditions Digest* and (in summary form) the *Survey of Current Business*.

The figures are available one month after the month to which they refer; they are revised in the subsequent 5 months as new source data become available. Annual revisions in the fall incorporate revised source data for earlier years. Comprehensive revisions affecting the content and methodology are made every 10 to 15 years.

Content

The LCLg system is based on the concept that profits are the prime mover of a private enterprise economy and that the recurring business cycles of expansion and recession are caused by changes in the outlook for profits. When the outlook for profits is positive, business expands production and investment, but when the outlook is negative, business retrenches. The outlook for profits is reflected in the LCLg system in the leading index and in the ratio of the coincident index to the lagging index, which is an alternative leading index.

The leading index represents business commitments and expectations regarding labor, product, and financial markets and, thus, points to future business actions. The coincident index represents the current level of actual production and sales, while the lagging index represents whether business costs are rising or falling. The ratio of the coincident to lagging index therefore suggests whether profits will rise or fall in the future due to the differential between sales and costs. If the coincident index increases faster than the lagging index, profits are likely to rise, and if the coincident index increases slower or declines in relation to the lagging index, profits are likely to fall. In this way, the coincident/lagging ratio is also a leading measure of trends in the economy.

Table 31 lists the component indicators included in the three indexes. The LEADING INDEX components reflect: the degree of tightness in labor markets due to employer hiring and firing; the buildup of orders, contracts, and inventories that affect future production; materials prices that reflect shortages or gluts of raw materials for which some time will be required to expand or

Table 31

Components of the LCLg Indexes

Leading Index

1. Average weekly hours of manufacturing production workers
   (*Average Weekly Hours*)
2. Average weekly initial claims for unemployment insurance
3. Manufacturers new orders for consumer goods and materials industries
   in 1982 dollars (*Manufacturers' Orders*)
4. Vendor performance (percent of companies receiving slower deliveries)
5. Contracts and orders for plant and equipment in 1982 dollars
6. New private housing building permits (*Housing Starts*)
7. Manufacturers unfilled orders for durable goods industries in 1982 dollars,
   monthly change (*Manufacturers' Orders*)
8. Prices of crude and intermediate materials, monthly change
   (*Producer Price Indexes*)
9. Stock prices of 500 common stocks (*Stock Market Price Indexes
   and Dividend Yields*)
10. Money supply (M-2) in 1982 dollars (*Money Supply*)
11. Index of consumer expectations (*Consumer Confidence Index and Consumer
    Statement Index*)

Coincident Index

1. Employees on nonagricultural payrolls (*Employment*)
2. Personal income less transfer payments in constant dollars
   (*Personal Income*)
3. Industrial production index (*Industrial Production Index*)
4. Manufacturing and trade sales in constant dollars

Lagging Index

1. Average duration of unemployment (*Unemployment*)
2. Inventory to sales ratio for manufacturing and trade in constant dollars
   (*Inventory-sales Ratios*)
3. Labor cost per unit of output in manufacturing, monthly change
   (*Unit Labor Costs*)
4. Commercial and industrial loans outstanding in constant dollars
   (*Bank Loans, Commercial and Industrial*)
5. Consumer installment credit outstanding to personal income ratio
   (*Consumer Installment Credit* and *Personal Income*)
6. Average prime rate charged by banks (*Interest Rates*)
7. Consumer price index for services, monthly change (*Consumer Price Index*)

reduce existing inventories; and financial conditions associated with the availability of funds in credit markets and the optimism and pessimism generated by price movements in the stock market. The COINCIDENT INDEX components reflect: employment; real incomes generated from production; output in cyclically sensitive manufacturing and mining industries; and real manufacturing and trade sales depicting the flow of goods from manufacturers to other consuming businesses, as well as to distributors and households. The LAGGING INDEX components reflect: the effect of the duration of unemployment on business costs of recruitment and training; the cost of maintaining inventories; labor cost per unit of output; the burden of paying back business and consumer loans; and interest payments as a cost of production.

The LCLg indexes are currently based on 1982 = 100.

Most, but not all, of the component indicators of the LCLg indexes are seasonally adjusted, but the three composite indexes are not seasonally adjusted at the overall level.

Methodology

The component indicators of the LCLg indexes are selected based on tests conducted for the following criteria: theoretical rationale for the leading, coincident, or lagging properties; differences in the timing of their change in direction in relation to the cyclical turning points of the overall economy; consistency with the general upward and downward direction of the business cycle; clear upward or downward trends as distinct from erratic monthly movements from which it is difficult to discern a trend; the quality of the survey used in collecting the data; promptness of the availability of monthly data; and the extent of revisions to preliminary data.

Data for the components of the LCLg indexes are based on many of the indicators discussed elsewhere in this book. These indicators are referenced in Table 31, although they are not always definitionally identical to the LCLg components.

The components are combined in the three indexes and weighted equally. Several statistical procedures are used in calculating the indexes. They include: (1) preventing the components that have sharp monthly movements from dominating the indexes; (2) smoothing short-term erratic movements of the components in order to better represent their cyclical patterns; and (3) setting the long-term growth trend of the indexes equal to the trend of real *gross national product*.

Accuracy

There are no estimates of sampling or revision error for the LCLg indexes. (Revision errors are provided for the leading index calculated by the Organization for Economic Co-operation and Development, as noted below.)

Relevance

The LCLg indexes help assess the current momentum and future direction of the economy. Because the coincident index reflects actual economic activity, it indicates whether the economy is currently expanding or in a recession. Movements in the leading index and the coincident/lagging ratio suggest whether the existing trend measured by the coincident index will continue. A change in direction in the leading index and the coincident/lagging ratio tends to foreshadow movement in the coincident index.

Figure 2 shows that the lead time between the change in direction of the leading measures and the coincident index is noticeably longer at the cyclical downturn than at the upturn. On average, over the business cycles since World War II, the leading index declines for 9 months and the coincident/lagging ratio declines for 13 months before the onset of a recession; by contrast, the lead time before the beginning of an expansion is 4 months for the leading index and 2 months for the coincident/lagging ratio. Changes in the lagging index follow the coincident index and are

Figure 2. **Leading, Coincident, and Lagging Indexes.**

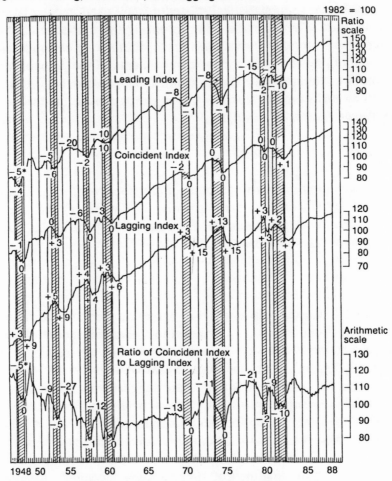

Notes: Based on Bureau of Economic Analysis data. Lined bars are recession periods. Numbers are monthly leads (−) and lags (+) from cyclical turning points.

* Not necessarily the peak but is the high for the available data.

thus used to confirm that a directional change has occurred. Because each cycle has unique characteristics, the advance signals of a pending recession in the leading index and the coincident/lagging ratio vary noticeably from expansion to expansion. Therefore, the average lead times noted above are only a rough guide for when a particular expansion will slide into a recession according to the LCLg system.

The LCLg indexes are a useful tool for forecasting the thrust of future economic trends. However, they are limited in that they do not directly forecast specific economic growth rates or the actual time of future cyclical turning points. (Specific forecasts are made indirectly using statistical regressions and analytic measures of rates of change in the leading and coincident indexes.) The LCLg indexes occasionally give false signals of a pending change in direction of the economy, such as prospective recessions in 1950–51, 1966, and 1984 that did not occur.

Recent Trends

Annual movements in the LCLg indexes are necessarily crude for identifying cyclical movements because they miss timing differences that occur between part of one year and part of the next year. Nevertheless, some common tendencies occur even in the context of calendar years.

Over the 1975–87 period, the leading index and the coincident/lagging ratio showed similar directional movements in all years, except 1985 and 1986; the leading index rose while the coincident/lagging ratio fell in those two years. Generally, the directional movements of both of these leading measures were accompanied by similar movements in the coincident index in the same or following year. The declines in the coincident index in 1975, 1980, and 1982 were all consistent with this pattern. However, in 1985 and 1986—when only the coincident/lagging ratio declined—the coincident index continued to rise. This suggests a recession is more likely to occur if both leading measures decline, rather than just one of them.

OTHER LEADING INDEXES

Leading indexes are also provided by other organizations: these include the Center for International Business Cycle Research of Columbia University (CIBCR), the Organization for

Economic Co-operation and Development (OECD), and the National Association of Purchasing Management (NAPM). The purpose of this section is to note their basic differences from the LCLg indexes should the reader wish to pursue them further.

The CIBCR and OECD measures are part of broader programs that provide leading indexes for the United States and several other nations. The CIBCR measures most closely resemble the LCLg indexes. They include all three indexes and have similar, but not identical, component items (including quarterly data that are interpolated to estimate an implied monthly movement).

The OECD measures are similar in overall concept to the LCLg indexes, but differ more in their implementation than the CIBCR. The OECD provides leading and coincident indexes but not lagging indexes. More of the component items differ from those in the LCLg, including industrial production which represents the highly cyclical industries as the sole component of the coincident index.

The NAPM composite index is the most dissimilar to the LCLg leading index. The NAPM does not provide coincident and lagging indexes. The NAPM index is limited to manufacturing industries which account for approximately 25 percent of the economy. (The LCLg leading index includes the entire economy.) The five components of the index are a mixture of leading and coincident indicators. However, because the statistical measures of the component items represent the proportion of companies in the NAPM survey reporting an increase (in purchasing) for the month and gives equal weight to small and large companies (referred to as a diffusion index), the coincident components have the property of leading indicators. (The LCLg component items are based on the total volume of activity reported by all companies.) The survey information in the NAPM index is based on a much smaller sample of respondents than the samples of the government surveys used in the LCLg system. The NAPM index uses differential weights for the components based on judgments about their importance. (While the NAPM index is officially published by NAPM, it was initially developed by the U.S. Department of Commerce, which still maintains and seasonally upates the index using NAPM survey data.)

Table 32

Leading, Coincident, and Lagging Indexes (annual percent change)

	Leading index	Coincident index	Lagging index	Coincident/ lagging ratio
1975	−5.1	−8.4	−7.1	−1.1
1976	13.8	7.0	−6.6	14.1
1977	5.0	6.9	2.5	4.3
1978	3.6	8.1	6.4	1.6
1979	−1.0	3.8	8.5	−4.2
1980	−4.2	−3.3	2.6	−5.5
1981	2.0	0.1	−2.5	2.4
1982	−1.2	−6.8	−2.8	−4.1
1983	16.2	1.8	−8.6	11.4
1984	4.8	10.2	10.2	0.1
1985	1.8	3.3	6.9	−3.4
1986	6.5	2.4	3.7	−1.3
1987	5.7	3.3	−0.1	3.5

References from Primary Data Sources

Bureau of Economic Analysis, U.S. Department of Commerce, *Handbook of Cyclical Indicators: A supplement to the Business Conditions Digest*, 1984.

Marie P. Hertzberg and Barry A. Beckman, "Business Cycle Indicators: Revised Composite Indexes," *Business Conditions Digest*, January 1989, and *Survey of Current Business*, January 1989.

Center for International Business Cycle Research, Graduate

School of Business, Columbia University, *International Economic Indicators*, monthly.

Ronny Nilsson, "OECD Leading Indicators," *OECD Economic Studies* (Organization for Economic Co-operation and Development), Autumn 1987.

Organization for Economic Co-operation and Development, *OECD Leading Indicators and Business Cycles in Member Countries, 1960–1985*, Sources and Methods No. 39, January 1987.

Theodore S. Torda, "Purchasing Management Index Provides Early Clue on Turning Points," *Business America*, U.S. Department of Commerce, June 24, 1985.

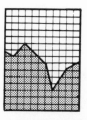 **MANUFACTURERS' ORDERS**

Manufacturers' orders measure commitments by customers to pay for subsequent delivery of goods produced by manufacturers. Orders are generally defined to be legally binding documents such as signed contracts, letters of award, or letters of intent, although there are exceptions. Orders figures are provided for new orders and for the backlog of unfilled orders.

Where and When Available

Measures of new orders and the backlog of unfilled orders for manufacturers' products are provided monthly by the Bureau of the Census in the U.S. Department of Commerce. They are published for durable and nondurable goods industries in the monthly report, *Manufacturers' Shipments, Inventories, and Orders*, and for durable goods industries only in *Advance Report on Durable Goods Manufacturers' Shipments and Orders*. Secondary sources include *Economic Indicators* and the *Survey of Current Business*.

The full report is available one month after the month to which the data refer. The advance report is available approximately five days earlier. The figures for the previous month are initially revised in every monthly report. These are subsequently revised based on annual benchmark information in March of the following year, and comprehensive benchmark revisions are made about every five years.

Content

New orders represent the dollar value of additional orders received each month for delivery during that month or later. They include contract changes that raise or lower the value of unfilled orders received in previous months. Unfilled orders represent, in dollar terms, the backlog of orders that have accumulated from previous months for goods that have not yet been delivered. They are a running total from one month to the next of the backlog at the beginning of the month, plus the new orders received during the month, and minus shipments of goods to customers and cancellations of existing orders during the month. The data on orders are broken down for durable and nondurable industries and for market categories of various consumer goods, capital goods, defense products, and materials.

The manufacturers' orders figures are seasonally adjusted.

Methodology

Manufacturers' orders figures are based on monthly surveys of manufacturers. These surveys also obtain information on shipments and inventories. While respondents are asked about both new and unfilled orders, the survey on new orders is incomplete. Due to the lack of readily accessible records, some survey respondents do not report new orders and others do not report new orders for goods that were shipped from existing inventories in the same month. Consequently, new orders are estimated indirectly from unfilled orders, shipments, and cancellations as follows:

	Unfilled orders (end of current month)*
plus:	Shipments (during month)
minus:	Unfilled orders (end of previous month)*
equals:	New orders (during month)

*Unfilled orders are net of cancellations during the month.

The survey sample of manufacturing companies originally included all companies with 1,000 or more employees and a probability sample of companies with 100–999 employees. Smaller companies are not included because of poor response rates in previous attempts to include them. The survey still has response problems: only about 55 percent of the companies with 1,000 or more employees respond. Overall, the survey sample accounts for about 50 percent of manufacturing shipments.

The monthly data are revised every year to reflect more complete information in the Annual Survey of Manufacturers. They are revised every five years to benchmark information in the Census of Manufacturers.

Accuracy

There are no estimates of sampling error for the manufacturers' orders figures. Revisions, based on annual figures and five-year benchmarking for new orders from 1982 to 1985, ranged from an increase of 2.8 percent in 1982 to a decrease of 2.6 percent in 1985. Revisions for end-of-year unfilled orders during the same period ranged from increases of 2.1 to 2.9 percent.

Relevance

Manufacturers' orders are significant because they indicate levels of demand and future levels of production and employment for manufacturing industries. There is a direct relationship between orders and production. Although determining when orders become production is not an exact science, rising orders are associated with higher current demand in the economy and subsequent increased production and employment, while falling orders indicate lower current demand followed by decreased production and employment. This relationship is true for both new and unfilled orders. However, new orders, which typically result in shipments of goods from existing inventories, are a good indicator of current levels of demand; unfilled orders are more closely linked to future production. Orders for market categories of certain consumer goods and materials in constant dollars are a component of the leading index of the *leading, coincident, and lagging indexes*.

The market category of capital goods is particularly significant because of its relation to *plant and equipment expenditures*. While capital goods orders are analogous in many ways to plant and equipment spending, several differences sometimes cause varying trends in the two figures. For example, capital goods orders cover only certain types of equipment that are made domestically, while plant and equipment spending includes structures and all equipment items whether produced domestically or imported. The two also differ in the dollar valuation and timing of the investment.

Table 33

Manufacturers' Orders
(billions of dollars)

	New orders	Unfilled orders (end of year)
1975	1,023	171
1976	1,194	180
1977	1,380	202
1978	1,579	257
1979	1,769	299
1980	1,874	320
1981	2,013	316
1982	1,947	310
1983	2,089	345
1984	2,277	368
1985	2,291	379
1986	2,264	382
1987	2,424	416

Recent Trends

New orders rose continuously through the late 1970s and then became volatile during the 1980s. After peaking at $2.0 trillion in 1981, they declined in 1982, rose through 1985, declined in 1986, and rose to $2.4 trillion in 1987.

Unfilled orders rose in the late 1970s and peaked at $320 billion in 1980. They declined to $310 billion in 1982 and then rose continuously to $416 billion in 1987.

Reference from Primary Data Source

Bureau of the Census, U.S. Department of Commerce, *Manufacturers' Shipments, Inventories, and Orders: 1982–1988*, August 1988.

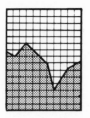

MONEY SUPPLY

The money supply measures represent the value of certain financial assets held by households, businesses, nonprofit organizations, and state and local governments. The types of assets included—which vary with each of the four money supply measures—are cash, bank deposits, money market instruments, federal securities, and trade credit notes. Financial assets such as stocks, commercial bonds, and life insurance, as well as all nonfinancial assets broadly defined as real estate and tangible goods, are excluded. The money supply therefore reflects assets which are very liquid and, consequently, are readily available for future spending.

Where and When Available

Money supply measures are provided weekly and monthly by the Federal Reserve Board. They are published in a statistical release and in the *Federal Reserve Bulletin*, the FRB's monthly magazine. Secondary sources include *Economic Indicators*, the *Survey of Current Business*, and *Business Conditions Digest*.

The weekly figures are available every Thursday for the week ending Monday of the previous week. The monthly figures are available in the middle of the month after the month to which they refer. The measures are revised on a continuing basis with the receipt of more accurate underlying data. The factors used to seasonally adjust the data are revised annually. Changes in the definitions since 1980 have been small.

Content

There are four alternative measures of the money supply—M–1, M–2, M–3, and L (liquid assets). In order, each measure represents an increasing number of financial assets. The measures progress from assets that are most liquid and most subject to Federal Reserve influence (M–1) to assets that are least liquid and least subject to Federal Reserve influence (L). Liquidity refers to how readily assets can be converted to cash with minimal loss in value. The Federal Reserve influences the growth rate of the money supply through buying and selling of federal securities in open market operations.

Table 34 shows the composition of assets covered by the four measures. Each measure following M–1 builds on the items in the previous one. For example, M–1 is composed of currency, demand deposits, and travelers checks. M–2 includes all of M–1 plus small savings accounts, money market holdings, overnight repurchase agreements, and Eurodollars. Similarly, M–3 is M–2 plus additional assets, and L is M–3 plus still more assets.

The money supply figures are seasonally adjusted.

Methodology

The money supply measures are based on data from several sources. The main sources are: demand, savings, and time deposits (from weekly reports of large commercial banks and quarterly reports of small and large commercial banks and savings and loan associations); money market mutual funds (from a survey by the Investment Company Institute); Treasury securities (from data supplied by the U.S. Department of the Treasury); commercial paper (based on data from brokers who deal in commercial paper and from firms that issue commercial paper directly); bankers' acceptances and term Eurodollars (from surveys by the Federal

Table 34

Money Supply Definitions
(billions of dollars)

	December 1987
M–1	$750.8
Currency (excludes bank-owned cash in bank vaults)	196.5
Demand (checking) deposits	288.0
NOW accounts (used for checking and saving)	259.3
Travelers checks, nonbank (e.g., American Express)	7.1
M–2	2,901.1
M–1	750.8
Small time deposits (less than $100,000) including open accounts and certificates of deposit	913.1
Savings deposits	414.3
Money market deposit accounts	525.2
Money market mutual funds (households, business, broker-dealers)	221.1
Overnight repurchase agreements (used in open market operations)	61.9
Overnight Eurodollars held by U.S. residents at overseas branches of U.S. banks	16.0
M–3	3,661.1
M–2	2,901.1
Large time deposits ($100,000 and more)	484.7
Term Eurodollars (maturities longer than 1 day)	90.8
Money market mutual funds (institutions only)	89.6
Term repurchase agreements (longer than 1 day)	105.5
L	4,323.9
M–3	3,661.1
Short-term Treasury securities (maturities less than 1 year, excluding savings bonds)	258.0
Commercial paper (unsecured promissory notes of well-known businesses)	258.9
Savings bonds (Treasury securities)	100.2
Bankers' acceptances (bankers agreements to pay bills of customers)	45.7

Note: The totals are seasonally adjusted but some components are not seasonally adjusted. The sums of the components do not equal the totals because certain adjustments are made at the total level to avoid double counting.

Reserve Bank of New York); and repurchase agreements and overnight Eurodollars (from Federal Reserve Board surveys of large banks). The weekly figures are derived from reports of large banks with trend estimates for small banks and other data sources. The monthly figures include a broader base of monthly reported data plus interpolated figures for data reported quarterly.

The data are adjusted to avoid double counting. For example, deposits of one bank held by another bank are excluded, as are assets held by money market mutual funds in other components of M-2, M-3, and L. In addition, estimates of float (checks credited to bank reserve accounts but not yet collected) are used to insure that all demand deposits are accounted for.

The money supply definitions were substantially revised in 1980 to reflect the growing impact of new financial instruments associated with monetary deregulation. Minor changes have been made since then.

Accuracy

There are no estimates of sampling or revision error for the money supply figures.

Relevance

Money supply trends are significant because of their effect on *interest rates*, real *gross national product*, and *inflation*. Generally, a rapid growth in the money supply tends to lower interest rates as lenders more actively seek borrowers as an outlet for their funds, and slow money supply growth raises interest rates as lenders have a smaller amount of funds available for loans. However, this relationship is sometimes reversed during periods of high inflation when rapid growth in the money supply is accompanied by higher interest rates because the money growth is perceived as fueling inflation through making more bank reserves available for loans.

The Federal Reserve uses the money supply figures as a major guide in formulating monetary policies to stimulate economic growth and moderate inflation. Under the Full Employment and Balanced Growth Act of 1978 (Humphrey-Hawkins Act), the Federal Reserve reports to Congress twice a year, in February and July, on its money supply targets for the current year. These reports indicate the targeted percentage increases in the money supply measures. The targets are presented as a range—for example, 5 to 8 percent—with the Federal Reserve exercising judgment in pursuing the upper or lower end of the range depending on the state of the economy. Targets typically are supplied for M-1, M-2, and M-3. However, because the relationship between M-1 and economic growth became more tenuous during the 1980s, M-1 targets weren't provided during the last years of the decade. Part of the diminution of the relationship between M-1 and economic growth is associated with the increasing volatility of M-1 discussed below under Recent Trends.

M-2 in constant dollars is a component of the leading index of *leading, coincident, and lagging indexes*.

Recent Trends

A striking example of how sharp changes in the money supply can influence interest rates occurred during the early 1980s. Beginning in late 1979, the Federal Reserve followed a deliberate policy through the summer of 1982 to slow money supply growth. They hoped this policy would lead to higher *interest rates* which would slow economic growth and thereby reduce *inflation*. Based on annual growth rates from December to December, there was a steady decline in M-1 growth from 8.3 percent in 1978 to 6.5 percent in 1981. As a result, interest rates climbed to the high teens, and in 1981–82 there was a deep recession and high *unemployment*. Consequently, the Federal Reserve reversed its policy and began accelerating money supply growth. Combined with lower inflationary expectations resulting from the recession, this led to lower interest rates and helped to stimulate economic growth. M-1 growth rose from 6.5

percent in 1981 to 9.6 percent in 1983.

There was considerable volatility in M–1 annual growth rates between 1983 and 1987. This reflects the greater availability of interest-paying demand deposits and NOW accounts associated with monetary deregulation. These assets allow greater investment opportunities for shifting assets between M–1 and the other kinds of money supply measures, depending on the level and movement of interest rates.

Table 35

Money Supply Measures
(annual percent change)

December to December	M–1	M–2	M–3	L
1975	4.9%	12.6%	9.5%	9.3%
1976	6.6	13.7	11.9	10.9
1977	8.0	10.6	12.3	12.4
1978	8.3	8.0	11.8	12.1
1979	7.7	8.0	9.7	10.9
1980	6.8	8.9	10.2	9.8
1981	6.5	9.9	12.3	11.7
1982	8.5	8.8	9.2	9.8
1983	9.6	11.8	10.2	10.6
1984	5.7	8.2	10.6	11.6
1985	12.4	8.4	7.3	8.7
1986	17.0	9.6	9.2	8.1
1987	3.5	3.3	4.9	4.6

References from Primary Data Source

"Recent Developments in Economic Statistics at the Federal Reserve: Part 2," *Business Economics*, National Association of Business Economists, July 1989. This article was written by the staff of the Federal Reserve Board.

Board of Governors of the Federal Reserve System, *The Federal Reserve System: Purposes and Functions*, 1984.

Thomas D. Simpson, "The Redefined Monetary Aggregates," *Federal Reserve Bulletin*, February 1980.

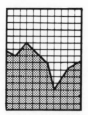

PERSONAL INCOME AND SAVING

Personal income (PI) mainly measures the income received by households from employment, self-employment investments, and transfer payments. It also includes small amounts for expenses of nonprofit organizations and income of certain fiduciary activities. Disposable personal income (DPI) refers to personal income after the payment of income, estate, and certain other taxes and payments to governments. Personal saving is the residual of DPI minus consumer outlays, and the saving rate is saving as a percent of DPI. The personal income and saving measures are definitionally consistent with those for the *gross national product*.

Where and When Available

Measures of personal income and saving are provided monthly by the Bureau of Economic Analysis in the U.S. Department of Commerce. The data are published in a monthly press release and in BEA's monthly magazine, the *Survey of Current Business*. Secondary sources include *Economic Indicators*, the *Federal Reserve Bulletin*, and *Business Conditions Digest*.

The dollar figures for PI, DPI, and personal saving are available during the third or fourth week of the month after the month to which they refer. These are revised initially in the subsequent two months. More detailed revisions are made annually every

July, and comprehensive benchmark revisions are made about every five years. Figures on the saving rate are available one month after the above noted dollar measures.

Content

PI mainly measures income of households. Household income is derived from wages, fringe benefits, self-employment, cash rent from rental housing, noncash rent imputed from owner-occupied homes, interest, dividends, social security and unemployment benefits, food stamps, and other income maintenance programs. PI also includes operating expenses (excluding depreciation) of not-for-profit organizations and investment income of life insurance companies and trust funds. PI reflects these income flows before the payment of income, estate, gift, and personal property taxes plus fees, fines, and penalties paid to federal, state, and local governments. Social security taxes paid by employees and employers are excluded from PI.

DPI is income excluding the tax and nontax payments to governments included in PI. DPI is provided in current and constant (1982) dollars.

Personal saving is the income remaining from DPI after deductions for consumer spending for goods and services (see *gross national product*), interest payments on consumer loans (excluding home mortgage interest), and money sent as gifts abroad (net transfer payments to foreigners). The saving rate is saving represented as a percent of DPI. In addition to savings deposits, money market deposit accounts, and certificates of deposits, saving figures include increases of household equity in housing and real estate investments and financial investments such as stocks and bonds, as well as reductions in consumer loans as the principal is paid off if the loans are financed from current income. Saving is reduced when consumers finance spending from existing savings or by selling real estate and financial assets to business, governments, or foreigners. Saving is not affected by gifts between households (such as when parents give a house to children) and by sales of homes, cars, and other assets between households (except for payments to intermediaries such as brokers' commissions and used car dealer markups).

The personal income and saving figures are seasonally adjusted.

Methodology

Data for the components of PI are obtained from several government and nongovernment sources with varying degrees of currency. For example, wages are based on the monthly *employment* payroll survey, and social security and unemployment benefit figures are based on monthly reports from the Social Security Administration and Department of Labor. Stock dividend income is derived from the Census Bureau's Quarterly Financial Report and from corporate quarterly reports to stockholders (these quarterly data are interpolated through the three months of the quarter in estimating the monthly figures). Data for other PI components, such as income from fringe benefits, self-employment, rent, interest, and life insurance benefits, typically are available only annually, and the monthly historical and current figures are mainly estimated indirectly.

DPI is calculated by subtracting income, estate, gift, and personal property taxes plus miscellaneous fines, fees, and penalties from PI. Data for these deductions are obtained from two sources. The Department of the Treasury provides monthly data for the federal component, and the Census Bureau provides a quarterly survey of state and local governments. However, the state and local survey data are used only in the historical quarterly figures because they are available too late for the current figures every quarter; indirect estimates are made for the current figures. DPI in constant dollars is calculated by dividing DPI in current dollars by the implicit price deflator for personal consumption expenditures (see *GNP price measures*).

Personal saving represents the difference between DPI and the sum of consumer spending for goods and services and interest payments on consumer loans (referred to as personal outlays). The saving rate for each month is calculated as a three-month moving average of saving as a percent of DPI in order to dampen erratic month-to-month movements. For this reason, the saving rate is published one month after the income and saving dollar figures.

Accuracy

There are no estimates of sampling or revision error for the personal income figures.

Relevance

PI represents the main component of consumer purchasing power and, thus, has a prime influence on consumer spending. Because consumer spending accounts for approximately 65 percent of the GNP, PI has a major effect on overall economic activity. DPI in constant dollars provides a better analytic measure of consumer purchasing power and its effect on real GNP than current-dollar personal income. Because personal saving indicates consumers' willingness to spend, the saving rate is an important predictor of future spending trends.

Recent Trends

PI, DPI, and DPI in constant dollars increased in all years during the 1975–87 period. However, the movements differed between the earlier and later years. PI rose more than DPI during 1975–81—92 percent compared to 86 percent; but this differential reversed slightly during 1981–87 when PI rose 50 percent and DPI rose 51 percent. In addition, DPI in constant dollars rose 39 percent over 1975–87, compared to 188 percent for PI and 181 percent for DPI.

The personal saving rate generally drifted downward during the thirteen-year period. From rates around 7 percent in the late

1970s, saving dropped to 4 percent in 1985 and 1986 and 3 percent in 1987.

Table 36

**Personal Income and Saving
(billions of dollars)**

	Personal income	Disposable personal income	Disposable personal income (1982 dollars)	Personal saving	Saving rate (percent)
1975	1,313.4	1,142.8	1,931.7	104.6	9.2%
1976	1,451.4	1,252.6	2,001.0	95.8	7.6
1977	1,607.5	1,379.3	2,066.6	90.7	6.6
1978	1,812.4	1,551.2	2,167.4	110.2	7.1
1979	2,034.0	1,729.3	2,212.6	118.1	6.8
1980	2,258.5	1,918.0	2,214.3	136.9	7.1
1981	2,520.9	2,127.6	2,248.6	159.4	7.5
1982	2,670.8	2,261.4	2,261.4	153.9	6.8
1983	2,838.6	2,428.1	2,331.9	130.6	5.4
1984	3,108.7	2,668.6	2,469.8	164.1	6.1
1985	3,325.3	2,838.7	2,542.8	125.4	4.4
1986	3,531.1	3,019.6	2,640.9	121.7	4.0
1987	3,780.0	3,209.7	2,686.3	104.2	3.2

References from Primary Data Source

Bureau of Economic Analysis, U.S. Department of Commerce, *State Personal Income: Estimates for 1929–82 and a Statement of Sources and Methods*, 1984.

Frank de Leeuw, ''Conflicting Measures of Private Saving,'' *Survey of Current Business*, November 1984.

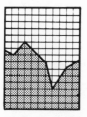

PLANT AND EQUIPMENT
EXPENDITURES

Plant and equipment (P & E) expenditures measure capital investment spending by private nonfarm business for new plant (buildings, roads, bridges, and other structures) and new equipment
(machinery, vehicles, furniture, and other items that last more
than one year). They include capital spending to expand existing
productive capacity and replace inefficient or outmoded capacity,
and cover spending for domestically produced as well as imported capital goods. They exclude capital spending by farm industries and governments and spending for housing and used P & E
facilities. The P & E expenditure figures are provided in current
and constant dollars.

Where and When Available

P & E expenditure figures for both historical and projected future
outlays are provided quarterly by the Bureau of the Census in the
U.S. Department of Commerce. (This program was transferred
from the Bureau of Economic Analysis in the Commerce Department to Census in 1988.) These data are published in a press
release. Secondary sources include *Economic Indicators*, the
Survey of Current Business, *Federal Reserve Bulletin*, and *Business Conditions Digest*.

The P & E spending figures are available in April, June,
September, and December, usually during the second week of the

month. The figures published in December project spending for the full calendar year ahead, and those for April, June, and September project spending for the balance of the year. Preliminary historical and projected future data are revised in succeeding quarters.

Content

The quarterly P & E figures cover companies in the mining, construction, manufacturing, transportation, communication, public utilities, trade, finance, insurance, and personal and business services industries. The sum of these quarterly figures is the typically cited total for "all industries." The annual total also includes data from the forestry, agricultural services, fishery, real estate, professional services, membership organizations, and social services industries, so that the annual total is cited as "total nonfarm business." The industry detail refers to the industry of the company that owns the P & E facilities, even though facilities may be leased and used by a company in another industry.

Expenditures are counted as occurring when payments to contractors and suppliers are made. Separate figures distinguishing plant from equipment are available annually.

The P & E figures are seasonally adjusted.

Methodology

The P & E expenditure figures are based on data from quarterly and annual surveys of private nonfarm business. The quarterly survey is based on a sample of approximately 12,000 profitmaking businesses, while the annual survey canvasses an additional 9,000 business and nonprofit organizations. Both the quarterly and annual surveys are based on nonprobability samples of these companies because of the difficulty of maintaining a representative sample of companies in various size categories for each industry.

The survey data are revised periodically to benchmark totals that are based on the five-year economic censuses, annual information available from Internal Revenue Service tax-related data in *Statistics of Income*, and other data from federal regulatory agencies. Companies in the sample for the quarterly survey represented 54 percent of all capital spending in 1977.

The spending projections include adjustments to the survey information for biases that have been observed in previous spending plan data. These bias adjustments raise or lower the projected survey data for each industry by the difference between actual and planned spending for the particular quarter based on experience of the past eight years. The constant-dollar historical P & E spending data are calculated by dividing the current-dollar survey data by implicit price deflators derived from unpublished figures associated with investment spending in the *gross national product*. The projected constant-dollar P & E figures are obtained by assuming that the rate of change of the deflator in the previous four quarters will continue for the coming year.

Accuracy

There are no estimates of sampling or revision error in the P & E figures. The average error in the projections over the 1955–83 period, without regard to whether the projection was above or below the actual spending, ranged from 1.8 percent for projections one quarter ahead to 3 percent for projections one year ahead.

Relevance

P & E expenditures affect the economy over both the short and the long term. Over the short term, investment spending generally has extreme cyclical movements, rising more during expansions and falling more during recessions than the overall economy, because investment is closely related to past and anticipated business profits. As the residual of sales minus costs, actual profits are intrinsically volatile, and anticipated profits are subject to business' changing optimistic and pessimistic perceptions of the future economic climate. This innate volatility is accentuated by the durability of existing P & E, which allows additional spending to be deferred until businesses believe it is a good time to obtain new facilities. Over the long term, P & E contributes to *productivity* because the use of more and better equipment tends to increase the nation's output.

Recent Trends

P & E spending rose continuously in the late 1970s and early 1980s, although at much lower rates of increase in 1980 and 1981. Spending was more volatile and increased more slowly in

Table 37

Plant and Equipment Spending by "All Industries"*
(billions of dollars)

	Current dollars	1982 dollars
1975	142.4	246.1
1976	158.4	255.1
1977	184.8	279.3
1978	217.8	304.4
1979	255.0	327.1
1980	282.8	332.7
1981	315.2	337.1
1982	310.6	310.6
1983	304.8	307.0
1984	354.4	358.0
1985	387.1	391.6
1986	379.5	376.2
1987	389.7	384.9

*Nonfarm industries surveyed quarterly. The broader measure of P & E spending for "total nonfarm business" that includes industries only surveyed annually as well as those surveyed quarterly was $440.7 billion in 1987, compared to $389.7 billion for industries surveyed quarterly.

the 1980s, declining in 1982 and 1983, rising in 1984 and 1985, declining in 1986, and rising in 1987.

Reference from Primary Data Source

Eugene P. Seskin and David F. Sullivan, "Revised Estimates of New Plant and Equipment Expenditures in the United States, 1947–83," *Survey of Current Business*, February 1985.

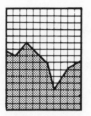

POVERTY

Measures of poverty count the number of persons or families with incomes below a specified minimum level. This income threshold defines subsistence living conditions according to current societal standards. Incomes below the threshold are regarded as subjecting the recipients to living conditions below currently accepted standards of decency. At any given point in time, the poverty level is defined as a specific income figure. However, what is regarded as the poverty level also has a relative dimension over longer periods of time. From the 1930s to the 1960s, the absolute value of the income threshold was raised as the nation changed its perceptions about what constitutes subsistence living. Standards typically are raised over time to reflect better living conditions afforded by advancements in technology. When the standard is raised, the number of persons defined as living in poverty increases. There are two measures of poverty: the official one counts cash income only; a supplementary one counts noncash in-kind transfer payments for food stamps, Medicare, and other income maintenance programs as well as cash income. The official measure defines more persons living in poverty than the supplementary one.

Where and When Available

The Bureau of the Census in the U.S. Department of Commerce provides annual measures of poverty. The figures are published annually in *Poverty in the United States, Money Income and Poverty Status of Families and Persons in the United States*, and *Estimates of Poverty Including the Value of Noncash Benefits*. Secondary sources include the *Economic Report of the President*.

The measures are available in the summer after the year to which they refer. Revisions for previous years are made in the annual publications.

Content

The poverty measures indicate the number of persons and families with incomes below the poverty income threshold. The official income threshold is based on the poverty standard developed by the Social Security Administration in 1964. Income requirements are differentiated for households depending on such characteristics as family size, age of the family members, and age of the family householder (householder is the person in whose name the home is owned or rented; when the home is jointly owned or rented by married couples either spouse's name may be used). The standard in the late 1980s reflects the same minimum living conditions specified when it was developed in 1964. It is routinely updated for inflation only, in order to maintain the 1964 living conditions. For example, the annual threshold income before taxes for a four-person family rose from $3,200 in 1964 to $11,600 in 1987. (There was no official poverty standard before 1964; as noted below under Relevance, there was an implied standard in the 1930s.)

Two alternative nonofficial poverty measures that include noncash as well as cash income are also provided. These measures treat in-kind noncash transfer payments as the equivalent of money in determining a family's income. One is based on the estimated market value (the price in the private market) of food stamps, Medicare and Medicaid, school lunches, and subsidized rental housing. The other is based on a more subjective concept of the estimated value of the benefit to the recipients (expenditures made on the benefit by unsubsidized households having the same income and other characteristics as subsidized households). Therefore, fewer people are counted as living in poverty under these definitions. For example, in 1987 the official measure shows 32.5 million persons living in poverty, compared to 20.4 million persons (market value) and 26.6 million persons (recipient value) when noncash transfer payments are counted as income.

Methodology

The poverty standard is based on estimates made by the U.S. Department of Agriculture in 1961 about how much money a three-or-more person family must have to meet minimal acceptable nutritional requirements under its economy food plan. This figure was multiplied by three to determine total income necessary to meet all living expenses, including housing, health, transportation, and all other nonfood items. This blowup factor is based on a 1955 study indicating that food accounts for one-third of the average household budget for families made up of three or more persons. Thus, the nonfood components are estimated indirectly as a statistical aggregate rather than by estimating each component separately with specific minimum standards for each.

The money income figures are based on the current population survey (CPS) conducted by the Census Bureau. The information is collected every March for the previous year. The survey sample is approximately 60,000 households, of whom typically 57,000 are interviewed and 3,000 are not available for interviews. For additional detail on the CPS, see *unemployment*.

The market value of the noncash items is estimated in different ways for each component: food stamp estimates reflect the actual dollar value in stores; Medicare and Medicaid estimates reflect the insurance value of health services which is calculated by dividing benefits paid to all noninstitutionalized persons covered in the health plans by all the persons covered in the plans (the estimates account for demographic distinctions by age and for disabled persons); public housing estimates reflect the difference between the private market value of the apartment and the rent paid by the tenant (considerable estimating is done for the private market value of the apartment); the school lunch estimates reflect the money and value of food commodities contributed by state governments and the U.S. Department of Agriculture to the program, exclusive of the money paid by students for the lunches.

Estimates of the recipient value of the noncash items are based on survey information of expenditures by nonsubsidized households, supplemented by a considerable amount of estimating. Because of the difficulty of estimating a recipient value for school lunches, the school lunch recipient value is the same as the market value.

Accuracy

The sampling error is that in 2 of 3 cases, the count of persons in poverty varies by approximately 500,000 and in 19 of 20 cases, the poverty count varies by 1,000,000.

Based on estimates derived from administrative records of income tax, unemployment insurance, social security, and other programs, survey respondents are considered to understate their income by approximately 10 percent in the aggregate for all sources of income. This overall underreporting is not taken into account when developing the poverty count because determining the amount of underreporting among income groups is difficult.

Relevance

The poverty measure reflects societal concerns about how well the nation is providing for the minimal subsistence needs of people at the bottom of the income ladder. It focuses attention on the most needy in the population and the progress made in alleviating their condition. As an absolute figure, it quantifies the magnitude of the poverty problem for purposes of political debate regarding appropriate ways to deal with it. Measures of the *distribution of income* are related to poverty.

Poverty is a relative concept that changes over time to reflect the economic aspirations of society. The poverty standard adopted in the early 1960s by President Lyndon Johnson is approximately 75 percent higher than the one used in the 1930s when President Franklin Roosevelt said one-third of the nation was ill-housed, ill-fed, and ill-clothed. Thus, perceptions of what constitutes a minimally acceptable standard of living changed signifi-

Table 38

Persons and Families Below the Poverty Income Level

	Persons		Families	
	Number (millions)	Percent of population	Number (millions)	Percent of population
1975	25.9	12.3%	5.5	9.7%
1976	25.0	11.8	5.3	9.4
1977	24.7	11.6	5.3	9.3
1978	24.5	11.4	5.3	9.1
1979	26.1	11.7	5.5	9.2
1980	29.3	13.0	6.2	10.3
1981	31.8	14.0	6.9	11.2
1982	34.4	15.0	7.5	12.2
1983	35.3	15.2	7.6	12.3
1984	33.7	14.4	7.3	11.6
1985	33.1	14.0	7.2	11.4
1986	32.4	13.6	7.0	10.9
1987	32.5	13.5	7.1	10.8

Persons Below the Poverty Income Level: Alternative Measures

	Money income* (millions)	Money and noncash income: market value (millions)	Money and noncash income: recipient value (millions)
1980	29.3	18.2	23.0
1985	33.1	21.9	27.2
1986	32.4	21.0	26.6
1987	32.5	20.4	26.6

*Official measure in above panel.

cantly over the 25-year period. The current standard has not been changed since the administration of President Johnson in the early 1960s. If it is raised based on a political consensus of higher minimal subsistence needs in the 1990s, the number of persons defined to be in poverty would increase. The federal budget deficit (*government budgets and debt*) operates as a major constraint to reviewing the standard. It is feared that even with noncash benefits included, a new standard would raise the poverty count and, thus, increase federal spending for income maintenance programs.

Recent Trends

The number of persons in poverty rose by 6.6 million over the 1975–87 period. The year-to-year movements reversed direction three times during the 12-year period. The poverty count declined from 1975 to 1978, rose from 1978 to 1983, declined from 1983 to 1986, and rose slightly in 1987. Persons living in poverty represented 13.5 percent of the population in 1987, up from 12.3 percent in 1975. Trends in the poverty rate during the period were similar to those for the absolute number of persons in poverty, except for a decline in 1987—down from 1975 to 1978, up from 1978 to 1983, and down from 1983 to 1987.

References from Primary Data Source

Bureau of the Census, U.S. Department of Commerce, *Poverty in the United States*, annual.

Bureau of the Census, U.S. Department of Commerce, *Money Income and Poverty Status of Families and Persons in the United States*, annual.

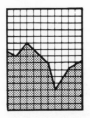

PRODUCER PRICE INDEXES

The producer price indexes (PPIs) track the rate of price change of domestically produced goods in the manufacturing, mining, agriculture, and electric utility industries. The PPIs most often used for economic analysis are the stage-of-processing indexes, composed of three independent indexes. The three are: finished goods; intermediate materials, supplies, and components; and crude materials for further processing. The three indexes are also consolidated into the all commodities index. By focusing on "goods," the PPIs exclude prices for construction and services.

Where and When Available

The PPIs are provided monthly by the Bureau of Labor Statistics in the U.S. Department of Labor. The data are published in a press release; in the BLS monthly magazine, the *Monthly Labor Review*; and in the report, *Producer Price Indexes*. Secondary sources include *Economic Indicators*, the *Survey of Current Business*, *Business Conditions Digest*, and the *Federal Reserve Bulletin*.

The figures are published approximately in the middle of the month immediately following the month to which they refer. The monthly figures are revised for the preceding fourth month—for example, revisions to January data are supplied in June with the release of May data. Annual revisions are usually made to the seasonally adjusted data for the preceding five years. Major revisions are made every ten years as part of comprehensive benchmarking. Current plans call for a comprehensive update of the weighting structure every five years.

Content

The three stage-of-processing PPIs have unique characteristics. FINISHED GOODS covers items used by a household, business, government, or foreign buyer in the form in which they were sold without further fabrication. These include household goods ranging from fresh foods to cars and capital goods such as tractors, trucks, and machine tools. INTERMEDIATE MATERIALS, SUPPLIES, AND COMPONENTS covers items that have been fabricated but are not ready for independent use and, thus, become part of other products, require further fabrication, or are otherwise used as inputs, such as cotton yarns, chemicals, containers, office supplies, electric power, and internal combustion engines. CRUDE MATERIALS FOR FURTHER PROCESSING covers items which are not sold directly to households and are either sold for the first time in their initial state of production, such as livestock or crude petroleum, or are being reused, such as scrap metal.

The three indexes reflect a theoretical typology of goods based on production, moving sequentially from a product's initial state to its end result. Classifying products by end user (household, business, government, or foreigner) and by degree of fabrication is referred to as stage-of-processing classification. Although the stage-of-processing concept theoretically represents a step-by-step flow from crude to intermediate to finished products, in practice this flow does not always occur. For example, there are reverse flows of intermediate containers to crude materials and of finished equipment to both the intermediate and crude material groups; there are also products which skip the intermediate stage, such as when crude live poultry becomes finished processed poultry.

Prices reflect the first sale of the goods by the producer and, thus, exclude price changes associated with resales and markups of the same item through wholesalers, retailers, or other producers. They represent the actual producer transaction price of goods meant for immediate delivery, including premiums and discounts from list prices and changes in the terms of sale such as distinctions for household and business customers and the size of the order. Prices of items with long production lead times are based on the time the item is delivered, not when the order was placed. The price quote is from the site of the producer (f.o.b., free-on-board), unless the price quote includes transportation charges when the producer provides such services directly and not through an outside transportation company or contractor. Exceptions to this include the use of list prices when transaction prices are not available (for example, fabricated steel products), and items bought on long-term contract when such contracts are the primary way of doing business (for example, coal). The indexes reflect price movements for the same or similar item exclusive of enhancement or reduction in the quality or quantity of the item. Prices on futures markets are excluded.

The PPIs are currently based on 1982 = 100.

The PPI figures are seasonally adjusted.

Methodology

Monthly price data are obtained from a mail survey conducted by the Bureau of Labor Statistics. The survey samples 22,000 companies in manufacturing and mining industries. The overall response rate to this survey is about 60 percent. These data are supplemented by price information provided by the U.S. Departments of Energy, Agriculture, and the Interior for prices of coal, electric power, and farm and fish products. Nearly all price quotes are reported by the sellers rather than the buyers.

The weights for each of the three PPIs are based on the value of sales of the component commodities. These reflect data in the five-year economic censuses, unless the industry is not covered in the censuses. For example, sales weights for electric power are based on Edison Electric Institute data. Since 1987, the weights represent 1982 sales volumes; during the previous ten years they were based on 1972 sales.

If the reported monthly price includes a change in the quality of the item, an adjustment is made to reflect the improvement or decline. Thus, the PPIs aim at measuring price movements of items having the same functional characteristics over time. For example, if better brakes are included on a car, the price increase attributable to the improved brakes does not appear as a price increase in the PPI, but if an auto bumper is weakened because of relaxed safety standards and there is no change in the market price, the weaker auto bumper is considered a price increase in the PPI. Because data to make the necessary adjustments are not always available, the PPI contains an unknown amount of price change caused by quality and quantity changes.

Accuracy

There are no estimates of sampling or revision error for the PPIs.

Relevance

The PPIs help assess rates of price change for goods at the production level. This is useful because production cost trends may differ from delivery and distribution costs. The PPIs provide a basis for analyzing whether *inflation* is caused by higher demand or by supply bottlenecks in the production of goods, independent of costs and markups associated with getting the goods to the buyer.

The stage-of-processing grouping in the PPIs also theoretically helps predict potential price changes in the sequential development of crude materials to intermediate materials to finished goods. However, the stage-of-processing concept does not establish a complete unidirectional flow of materials in the production process from crude to intermediate to finished goods. While theoretically, crude prices should predict intermediate prices, and intermediate prices should predict finished prices, these lead-lag relationships are not exact because of the failure to maintain a unidirectional flow in the stage-of-processing groups. More research on the properties of these classifications is needed to realize their analytic potential.

The PPIs also are used to determine cost escalation in business contracts and to deflate the *gross national product* to constant dollars.

Recent Trends

Inflation based on the PPIs accelerated in the late 1970s, reaching a peak annual increase of 13.5 percent in 1980 for finished goods and 15 percent for intermediate products, while inflation in crude materials peaked in 1979 at 17 percent. There was a subsequent slowdown in inflation including actual price declines. Generally,

Table 39

**Producer Price Indexes
(annual percent change)**

	Finished goods	Intermediate materials, supplies, and components	Crude materials for further processing
1975	10.8%	10.5%	0.4%
1976	4.4	5.1	2.9
1977	6.5	6.6	3.2
1978	7.8	7.0	12.0
1979	11.1	12.8	17.0
1980	13.5	15.3	11.0
1981	9.2	9.2	8.1
1982	4.1	1.4	−2.9
1983	1.6	0.6	1.3
1984	2.1	2.5	2.2
1985	1.0	−0.4	−7.4
1986	−1.4	−3.5	−8.5
1987	2.1	2.4	6.7

inflation hovered around 2 percent during the 1982–87 period, although there were noticeable price declines in 1985 and 1986, and a sharp increase in crude materials prices in 1987.

During this 13-year period, prices of intermediate materials and finished goods tended to move in parallel, while crude materials had more distinctive year-to-year patterns. Prices of crude materials also were more volatile than those for intermediate materials and finished goods. Some of these differences result from fluctuations of oil prices, which have their initial and heaviest impact on crude materials. The effect of the price of oil is successively dampened as an increasing number of nonpetroleum prices are incorporated in the intermediate and finished categories.

References from Primary Data Source

Bureau of Labor Statistics, U.S. Department of Labor, *BLS Handbook of Methods*, April 1988, Chapter 16.

Andrew G. Clem and William D. Thomas, "New weight structure being used in Producer Price Index," *Monthly Labor Review*, August 1987.

Sarah Gousen, Kathy Monk, and Irvin Gerduk, *Producer Price Measurement: Concepts and Methods*, Bureau of Labor Statistics, U.S. Department of Labor, June 1986.

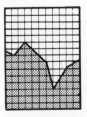

PRODUCTIVITY

Productivity represents the nation's efficiency in producing goods and services. It is estimated as output per unit of input. There are two measures of productivity. Labor hour productivity, which is the traditional measure, encompasses the labor and capital equipment used in production as well as factors affecting their efficiency, such as worker and management skills, worker effort, technology, and energy and materials usage. Multifactor productivity focuses solely on the factors affecting the efficiency of labor and capital facilities—worker and management skills, technology, etc.

Where and When Available

LABOR HOUR PRODUCTIVITY. This measure of productivity for broad economy-wide sectors and the total of all manufacturing industries is provided on a quarterly basis by the Bureau of Labor Statistics in the U.S. Department of Labor. The data are published in a press release and in two BLS monthly magazines, the *Monthly Labor Review* and *Employment and Earnings*. Secondary sources include *Economic Indicators* and *Business Conditions Digest*. Another set of labor hour productivity measures, covering specific industries and based on different definitions from the economy-wide measures, is published annually in *Productivity Measures for Selected Industries and Government Services*.

Preliminary data for the immediately preceding quarter are provided in the second month following the quarter (May for the first quarter, August for the second quarter, November for the third quarter, and February for the fourth quarter). The data are available at the same time as the *unit labor cost* figures and follow soon after publication of the *gross national product* measures. The data are initially revised in the subsequent two months. Annual revisions are made every September, and still more comprehensive benchmark revisions are made about every six years.

MULTIFACTOR PRODUCTIVITY. This measure of productivity for broad economy-wide sectors and the total of all manufacturing industries is provided annually by the Bureau of Labor Statistics in the U.S. Department of Labor. The data are published in a press release. The figures are available in October for the preceding year. There are no revisions for earlier years. Another set of multifactor productivity measures, covering specific industries and based on different definitions from the economy-wide measures, is published every one to two years.

Content

LABOR HOUR PRODUCTIVITY. This measure is defined as output per hour of labor expended. Output per hour encompasses the combined influences of all factors affecting the use of labor, such as *plant and equipment expenditures*, the substitution of plant and equipment for labor, worker skills and effort, technology, managerial skills, level of output, *capacity utilization,* energy and materials usage, and the interactions among them. By excluding labor hours, labor hour productivity also excludes the effect on output of labor hours. The productivity measure does not separate the specific contributions to productivity of labor, capital, or any other element. Labor hour productivity is typically expressed as an index, although absolute figures in constant dollars also are available.

Separate estimates are developed for the business sector, the nonfarm business sector, and the total of all manufacturing industries. They are based on real *gross national product* data adjusted to eliminate those components of the GNP that would cause an inappropriate measure of productivity because (a) the output indicator used is also an input measure or (b) the output and input data are inconsistent. The business sector figures cover private for-profit enterprise and government enterprise. They exclude not-for-profit organizations; general government (general government is financed mainly by taxes while government enterprises are financed mainly by user fees); household employment; owner-occupied housing; and profit flows of American companies abroad into the U.S. The nonfarm business sector figures also exclude farming.

The output definitions of the three economy-wide measures are based on the value added concept of the GNP. This method counts output as the sum of labor, profits, interest, depreciation allowances, and indirect business taxes, but excludes purchased materials and services. By contrast, output measures for the specific industries include both value added and purchased materials and services.

The labor hour productivity indexes are currently based on 1977 = 100.

The labor hour productivity figures are seasonally adjusted.

MULTIFACTOR PRODUCTIVITY. This measure estimates efficiency as output per unit of labor and capital combined. It is the component of labor hour productivity that focuses on the underlying efficiency and external conditions of production operations. These include labor skills and worker effort, technology, managerial skills, level of output, *capacity utilization*, energy and materials usage, and the interactions among them. Labor hour productivity includes these items plus plant and equipment usage and the substitution of plant and equipment for labor. By excluding from labor hour productivity both labor hours and *plant and equipment expenditures*, multifactor productivity also excludes the effect on output of the substitution of plant and equipment for labor. The figures are provided as an index.

As in the case of labor hour productivity, separate multifactor figures are developed for the business sector, the nonfarm business sector, and the total of all manufacturing industries, which are based on the *gross national product* value-added definitions of output. Also following labor productivity, output definitions for the multifactor figures for specific industries include both value added and purchased materials and services.

The multifactor productivity indexes are currently based on 1977 = 100.

Methodology

LABOR HOUR PRODUCTIVITY. Productivity is defined as the ratio of output (the numerator) to input (the denominator). Output is represented by either the *gross national product* business sectors or the total of all manufacturing industries, and input is represented by the corresponding labor hours. This leaves the sum total of all capital and multifactor elements as the items affecting the efficiency of labor. Labor hours are the product of *employment* multiplied by *average weekly hours* converted to average annual hours. The employment data are based on the sum of paid jobs counted in the payroll survey and the number of self-employed and unpaid family workers counted in the household survey (see *employment*).

$$\text{Labor hour productivity} = \frac{\text{Output}}{\text{Input}} = \frac{\text{Real GNP* (or manu-facturing)}}{\text{Labor hours**}} = \text{Real output per labor hour}$$

*Business sector or nonfarm business sector.
**Paid employees, the self-employed, and unpaid family workers.

MULTIFACTOR PRODUCTIVITY. This measure is also a ratio of output to input. The output figure in the numerator is the same as used above for labor hour productivity. The input figure in the denominator is the weighted average of the dollar value of labor hours and of capital services from plant and equipment, land, and inventories. This leaves the sum total of all multifactor elements—worker and management skills, technology, etc.—as the items affecting the efficiency of labor and capital resources.

$$\text{Multifactor productivity} = \frac{\text{Output}}{\text{Input}} = \frac{\text{Real GNP (or manufacturing)}}{\text{Labor hours and capital services}} = \text{Output per unit of labor and capital services}$$

NEW DEFINITION OF LABOR HOURS. The definition of labor hours in the above discussion was changed in mid-1989. Until then, labor hours were based on "hours paid," which includes time at the job site and time on paid vacation and sick leave. Beginning in mid-1989, labor hours are based on "hours at work" which is limited to time at the job site, and thus excludes time associated with paid vacation and sick leave. The new definition changes productivity movements slightly, but doesn't affect basic patterns over the years. The data in Table 40 are based on the old hours paid definition because, when this book went to press, revised data for previous years were available for labor hour productivity but not yet for multifactor productivity.

Accuracy

LABOR HOUR PRODUCTIVITY. In 19 of 20 cases, the second quarterly revision (two months after the preliminary figure) differs from the preliminary index by plus or minus 2 index points.

MULTIFACTOR PRODUCTIVITY. There are no estimates of sampling or revision error.

Relevance

LABOR HOUR PRODUCTIVITY. Productivity is important because greater efficiency increases the quantity of goods and services available for civilian and defense needs. The relationship of productivity to *inflation*, *average weekly earnings*, and *employment* is also important. When productivity increases rapidly, more goods and services are available at lower prices because of lower production costs. High productivity growth permits higher wages without increasing production costs and inflation.

High productivity can cause employment dislocation, however, because the introduction of new technology changes or eliminates some jobs. Displaced workers with outmoded skills may not be able to find new jobs or may only find work at lower rates of pay. While some individuals may therefore be adversely affected by higher productivity, higher productivity does not lead to *unemployment* or lower wages at the economy-wide level. The greater incomes and lower prices attributable to productivity growth cause overall spending and employment to increase.

Because quarterly movements of productivity are heavily influenced by cyclical changes in output, short-term changes in productivity mainly reflect cyclical changes in economic activity rather than basic changes in efficiency. Such basic changes are discerned by examining trends over at least several quarters that have relatively steady rates of economic growth. Over the longer run, the basic changes are seen more directly in the annual movements in multifactor productivity noted below.

MULTIFACTOR PRODUCTIVITY. This measure of underlying productivity suggests the extent to which labor, capital, materials, and other aspects of production are improving, both in terms of technology and in efficient usage. Changes in multifactor productivity indicate fundamental changes are occurring that impact productivity. However, because multifactor productivity encompasses all of the causal factors, further analysis is necessary to identify which elements are changing significantly.

Recent Trends

Productivity in the business sector generally showed a decelerating rate of increase or actual decline during the 1975–82 period. Productivity rose at an increasing rate in 1983–84, with the rate of increase slowing during 1985–87. In manufacturing, productivity increased at a decelerating rate or declined during 1975–80, generally rose at increasing rates during 1981–84, and increased more slowly during 1985–87. These patterns were similar for both the labor hour and multifactor productivity measures.

Table 40

**Productivity
(annual percent change)**

	Business sector		Manufacturing	
	Labor hour	Multifactor	Labor hour	Multifactor
1975	2.0%	−0.5%	2.5%	−1.4%
1976	2.8	3.0	4.6	5.2
1977	1.6	2.1	3.0	3.2
1978	0.8	1.2	1.5	1.6
1979	−1.2	−1.6	−0.1	−0.7
1980	−0.4	−2.2	0.0	−2.3
1981	1.4	0.3	2.2	1.1
1982	−0.3	−2.5	2.2	−0.5
1983	2.8	2.5	5.8	5.9
1984	2.5	3.4	5.5	6.8
1985	2.1	1.4	4.6	3.8
1986	2.2	1.5	3.3	3.7
1987	0.8	0.8	3.4	3.4

References from Primary Data Source

Bureau of Labor Statistics, U.S. Department of Labor, *BLS Handbook of Methods,* April 1988, Chapters 10 and 11.

Jerome A. Mark, William H. Waldorf, et al, *Trends in Multifactor Productivity, 1948–81*, Bulletin 2178, Bureau of Labor Statistics, U.S. Department of Labor, September 1983.

Jerome A. Mark, "Problems encountered in measuring single- and multifactor productivity," *Monthly Labor Review*, December 1986.

William Gullickson and Michael J. Harper, "Multifactor productivity in U.S. manufacturing, 1949–83," *Monthly Labor Review*, October 1987.

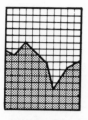

STOCK MARKET PRICE INDEXES AND DIVIDEND YIELDS

Common stock is the ownership instrument of American corporations. Holders of common stock are risk-taking investors who share in the profits if dividends are paid. Rising and falling stock prices affect capital gains and losses to investors. The current rate of return on a share of common stock—also referred to as the dividend yield—is the percent that annual dividends are of the market price.

Where and When Available

The four stock market price indexes covered here are provided daily by the New York Stock Exchange, Inc.; Standard & Poor's Corporation; Dow Jones & Co., Inc.; and Wilshire Associates. They are published in daily newspapers, *Barron's*, and Standard and Poor's *Standard & Poor's Indexes of Security Markets* and *Current Statistics*. Secondary sources include *Economic Indicators*, the *Survey of Current Business*, and *Business Conditions Digest*.

The indexes are also disseminated electronically every minute during the trading day by the New York Stock Exchange and commercial stock quote services, except for the Wilshire index which is available only for the closing at the end of the day.

Content

Two of the common stock price indexes represent different groups of publicly held companies traded on the New York Stock Exchange, and two include the American Stock Exchange and the Over-the-Counter market as well as the New York Stock Exchange. The effect of changes in the capitalized financial structure of companies such as stock splits, mergers, and spin-offs is eliminated from the indexes so that price movements are not distorted by changes in the underlying value of a share of stock following a new capitalization of the company. Therefore, the index levels cannot be compared to an average of actual current market prices for the same companies because the latter would reflect the effect of new capitalizations on the price per share without adjusting for changes in the underlying value of each share.

The stock market price indexes are not seasonally adjusted.

NEW YORK STOCK EXCHANGE COMPOSITE INDEX. This index covers prices of all of the over 1,500 companies listed on the New York Stock Exchange. The index reflects the change in the price of an average share of stock of companies since December 31, 1965, when the average market value was approximately $50. Component indexes of the composite are provided for companies in the industrial, transportation, utility, and finance groups.

DOW JONES INDUSTRIAL AVERAGE. This index covers prices of 30 companies listed on the New York Stock Exchange. They are widely held large "blue chip" companies that are mainly in manufacturing industries, but also include mining, communications, finance, and retail firms. They account for approximately 25 percent of the market value of all companies on the New York Stock Exchange and 20 percent of the market value of the over 5,000 companies traded on all U.S. stock exchanges in the mid-1980s. The average reflects the price of an average share of stock based on the capitalized structure of companies when they were first incorporated in the index. Other Dow-Jones indexes are provided for transportation and utility companies and for the composite index of 65 industrial, transportation, and utility companies.

STANDARD & POOR'S 500 COMPOSITE PRICE INDEX. This index covers prices of 500 companies listed on the New York Stock Exchange, American Stock Exchange, and the Over-the-Counter market. Of the total index, companies on the New York Stock Exchange account for 97.0 percent of the market value, the American Stock Exchange for 2.3 percent, and Over-the-Counter for 0.7 percent. They include large and medium-size companies, and account for 58 percent of the market value of the over 5,000 stocks traded on all U.S. stock exchanges in 1987. The index reflects the price of an average share of common stock based on the capitalized structure of companies during 1941–43, when the average market value was $10. Component indexes of the 500 composite are provided for companies in the industrial, transportation, utilities, and financial groups. Supplementary indexes based on different categories of products and stock are available for companies in the consumer and capital goods industries, high-grade common stocks, and low-priced common stocks.

WILSHIRE 5000 EQUITY INDEX. This index covers prices of over 6,000 companies including all New York Stock Exchange and American Stock Exchange listed companies plus all Over-the-Counter companies traded on the National Association of Securities Dealers Automated Quote System. The "5000" in the title has become outdated as the index has expanded to over 6,000 companies. The index reflects the market value based on the capitalized structure of companies as of December 31, 1980, when the market value was $1,404.596 billion (the base index is 12/31/80 = 1,404.596). It is the most comprehensive measure of common stock values traded in major markets. Of the total index, companies on the New York Stock Exchange account for approximately 86 percent of the market value, the American

Stock Exchange for 3 percent, and Over-the-Counter for 11 percent.

DIVIDEND YIELDS. The dividend yield for the four stock market price indexes is based on cash dividends only (stock dividends are excluded).

Methodology

As noted above, the four common stock price indexes are adjusted to eliminate the price effect of changes in the capitalized financial structure of companies, such as stock splits, mergers, and spin-offs. This maintains the capitalized structure of each company as it was when the company was included in the index. The New York Stock Exchange, Standard & Poor's, and Wilshire indexes are weighted using the market value of the companies in the index as weights. The market value of a company is the number of its common stock shares outstanding multiplied by the price per share. The Dow Jones index is weighted using the price per share of the companies in the index as weights.

NEW YORK STOCK EXCHANGE COMPOSITE INDEX. The index indicates the percent change in the market value of all listed stocks on the New York Stock Exchange between the base period (December 31, 1965) and the current period. The percent change in the market value from the base period to the current period multiplied by 50 gives the current index. The number 50 is close to the average price of all stocks in the base period. The stocks are averaged proportionate to the market values of each company, which gives price movements of firms with large market values more weight than those with small market values. New companies are added and old companies are deleted from the index as the companies are listed and delisted on the New York Stock Exchange.

DOW JONES INDUSTRIAL AVERAGE. The index indicates the average price per share of 30 stocks on the New York Stock

Exchange. The stocks are averaged arithmetically according to the price per share of each company, which gives more weight to price movements of companies with high prices per share than those with low prices per share. New companies are substituted for old companies mainly because of mergers, but also to update the index to better represent large widely held companies.

STANDARD & POOR'S 500 COMPOSITE PRICE INDEX. The index represents the percent change in the market value of 500 stocks on the New York Stock Exchange, American Stock Exchange, and the Over-the-Counter market between the base period (1941–43) and the current period. The selection of companies for inclusion in the index is based on an assessment of the following factors: position in the industry, market value size, distribution of shares among shareholders, trading volume, emerging companies or industries, and stock price movements. The percent change in the market value from the base period to the current period multiplied by 10 gives the current index. The number 10 is the assigned market value for the base period. The stocks are averaged proportionate to the market values of each company, which gives price movements of firms with large market values more weight than those with small market values. New companies are substituted for old companies because of mergers and bankruptcies and to update the representation of stocks to more closely reflect the composition of companies in the industrial, transportation, utilities, and financial groupings of the New York Stock Exchange Composite Index.

WILSHIRE 5000 EQUITY INDEX. The index indicates the percent change in the market value of all listed stocks on the New York Stock Exchange and American Stock Exchange plus the Over-the-Counter companies traded in the National Association of Security Dealers Automated Quote System (NASDAQ) between the base period (December 31, 1980) and the current period. The percent change in the market value from the base period to the current period multiplied by 1,404.596 gives the current index. The number 1,404.596 represents the market value in the base period. The stocks are averaged proportionate to the market values of each company, which gives price movements of firms with large market values more weight than those with small market values. New companies are added and old companies are deleted from the index as the companies are listed and delisted on the New York and American Stock Exchanges and on the NASDAQ.

NEW YORK STOCK EXCHANGE COMPOSITE DIVIDEND YIELD. The dividend yield is the percent that the annualized quarterly cash dividends are of the current market value of the stocks at the end of the quarter (methodology adopted in 1985). The annual dividend yield is the average of the four quarters. (Before 1985, dividends represented a moving average of annualized dividends of the most recent four quarters; the dividend yield was the percent this four-quarter average was of the current market value of the stocks at the end of the quarter.)

DOW JONES INDUSTRIAL AVERAGE DIVIDEND YIELD. Dividends represent a moving average of annualized dividends of the most recent four quarters, and the dividend yield is the percent this four-quarter average is of the current market value of the stocks at the end of the quarter. The annual dividend yield is the average of the four quarters.

STANDARD & POOR'S 500 COMPOSITE DIVIDEND YIELD. The dividend yield is the percent that the annualized quarterly cash dividends are of the current market value of the stocks at the end of the quarter. The annual dividend yield is the average of the four quarters.

WILSHIRE 5000 EQUITY DIVIDEND YIELD. The dividend yield is the percent that the actual monthly cash dividends are of the current market value of the stocks at the end of the month. This is much lower than an annualized dividend yield. The annual dividend yield is the sum of the yields for the 12 calendar months.

Accuracy

There are no estimates of sampling or revision error for the stock market price indexes and dividend yields. The New York Stock Exchange Composite Index and the Wilshire 5000 Equity Index are based on the universe of firms and, thus, are not subject to sampling error.

Relevance

Stock prices influence the course of future economic activity because they affect the *consumer confidence index* and *consumer sentiment index* and *plant and equipment expenditures*. High or rising stock prices encourage consumer and investment spending because they promote optimism about the economy. Low or falling stock prices discourage such spending because of the pessimistic outlook they foster. The Standard and Poor's 500 Composite Price Index is a component of the leading index of the *leading, coincident, and lagging indexes*.

Stock prices affect consumer spending because of the effect of stocks on personal wealth. Households feel richer and more willing to spend when the value of their paper stockholdings is high than when the value of their stockholdings is low. Stock prices also influence investment spending because high stock prices make it easier for businesses to finance new investment by selling new equity stock or by obtaining loans through new bond sales or other debt financing. The choice of equity or debt financing is determined by differences in the cost of raising funds (dividends on stock vs. interest on bonds) and by the effect of selling new stock on the ownership control of the company. Generally, it is easier to sell new stock when stock prices are high or rising than when they are weak.

Dividend yields implicitly incorporate investor perceptions of future trends in stock prices. Low yields suggest expectations of large or long-term price increases, and high yields indicate anticipated small price increases or long-term price declines. Dividend

Table 41

Common Stock Price Indexes and Dividend Yields

Price Indexes

	New York Stock Exchange Composite Index (12/31/65 = 50)	Dow Jones Industrial Average	Standard & Poor's 500 Composite Price Index (1941–43 = 10)	Wilshire 5000 Equity Index (12/31/80 = 1,405.596)
1975	45.73	802.49	82.16	763.756
1976	54.46	974.92	102.01	903.048
1977	53.69	894.63	98.20	892.062
1978	53.70	820.23	96.02	913.278
1979	58.32	844.40	103.01	1,028.862
1980	68.10	891.41	118.78	1,229.610
1981	74.02	932.92	128.05	1,340.827
1982	68.93	884.36	119.71	1,239.631
1983	92.63	1,190.34	160.41	1,691.623
1984	92.46	1,178.48	160.46	1,640.776
1985	108.09	1,328.23	186.84	1,945.067
1986	136.00	1,792.76	236.34	2,441.717
1987	161.70	2,275.99	286.83	2,831.136

Annual Percent Change

1975	4.3%	5.7%	4.0%	7.1%
1976	19.1	21.4	18.4	18.2
1977	-1.4	-8.2	-3.7	-1.2
1978	0.1	-8.3	-2.2	2.3
1979	8.6	2.9	7.3	12.7
1980	16.8	5.6	15.3	19.5

1981	8.7	4.7	7.8	9.0
1982	−6.9	−5.2	−6.5	−7.5
1983	34.4	34.6	34.0	36.5
1984	−0.2	−1.0	0.03	−3.0
1985	16.9	12.7	16.4	18.5
1986	25.8	35.0	26.5	25.5
1987	18.9	27.0	21.4	15.9

Dividend Yields
(percent)

	New York Stock Exchange Composite Index	Dow Jones Industrial Average	Standard & Poor's 500 Composite Index	Wilshire 5000 Equity Index
1975	4.6%	4.7%	4.3%	4.3%
1976	4.6	3.9	3.8	4.0
1977	5.7	5.1	4.6	4.6
1978	5.9	5.8	5.3	5.0
1979	6.2	5.9	5.5	5.2
1980	5.4	6.0	5.3	4.8
1981	6.7	6.1	5.2	5.0
1982	5.2	6.3	5.8	5.1
1983	4.4	4.5	4.4	4.0
1984	4.5	4.9	4.6	4.3
1985	3.6*	4.5	4.3	4.2
1986	3.4	3.6	3.5	3.2
1987	3.4	3.1	3.1	3.0

*Because of a change in methodology in 1985, the figures since 1985 are not fully comparable to those of earlier years.

yields also affect patterns of investment. Thus, low yields may drive investors out of stocks into bonds, real estate, or other opportunities that have an expected higher return, while high yields may entice investors into stocks, both because of the high return and the anticipation that the high yield will stimulate higher stock prices.

The Standard & Poor's 500 Composite Index is traded as a futures option on the Chicago Mercantile Exchange.

Recent Trends

Stock prices rose in 9 to 10 of the 13 years over the 1975–87 period (depending on the index), with declines or stability occurring in 1977, 1978, 1982, and 1984. From 1975 to 1987, the Wilshire 5000 Equity Index had the highest growth (271 percent), and the Dow Jones Industrial Average had the lowest growth (184 percent). The New York Stock Exchange Composite Index (254 percent) and the Standard & Poor's 500 Composite Index (249 percent) were closer to the high growth of the Wilshire than to the low growth of the Dow-Jones. There was also a greater similarity among the year-to-year movements of the Wilshire, New York Stock Exchange, and Standard & Poor's indexes than of the Dow Jones index.

Dividend yields generally rose from 4 to 4.5 percent in 1975–76 to 5 to 6 percent during 1979–82 (the New York Stock Exchange yield was 6.7 percent in 1981). They subsequently declined during the 1980s to lows of 3 to 3.5 percent in 1986 and 1987. Variations in yields among the four indexes were usually within 0.5 of a percentage point, although larger differences occurred during 1979–81 and 1985. The New York Stock Exchange and the Dow Jones indexes typically had the highest yield and the Wilshire index typically had the lowest.

Price and dividend behavior of large long-established companies differs from that of small new companies. This is highlighted in the noticeable differences between the Dow Jones index which concentrates on blue chip companies and the Wilshire index which represents the broadest spectrum of American business, including small new companies. Comparisons of the various indexes are useful for determining whether sharp movements in stock market prices are driven by a limited group of companies or if they are broadly based.

References from Primary Data Sources

New York Stock Exchange, Inc., Options and Index Products Division, and New York Futures Exchange, Inc., *NYFEline & Outlook*, 1988.

Dow Jones & Co., Inc., *Dow Jones Averages: A Non-Professional's Guide*, revised edition, 1986.

Standard & Poor's Corporation, "Special Supplement: Standard & Poor's Stock Price Indexes—Description of Method Used in Compilation," *S & P "500" Information Bulletin*, January 1988.

Albert S. Neubert, "The S & P 500," *American Association of Individual Investors (AAII) Journal*, January 1987.

Wilshire Associates, "Wilshire 5000 Notes."

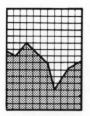

UNEMPLOYMENT

Unemployment counts the number of persons without jobs who are available for and actively seeking work. It covers all persons 16 years and older who lost or quit previous jobs as well as school graduates, students, and others with no work experience or who re-enter the workplace. The unemployment rate is the percentage that unemployed persons are of the labor force, and the labor force is defined as the sum of the employed and unemployed. As a relative measure of additional workers available for employment, the unemployment rate reflects the slack or tightness in labor markets.

Where and When Available

Unemployment measures are provided monthly by the Bureau of Labor Statistics in the U.S. Department of Labor. The data are published in a press release and in two BLS monthly magazines, the *Monthly Labor Review* and *Employment and Earnings*. Secondary sources include *Economic Indicators*, the *Survey of Current Business*, *Business Conditions Digest*, and the *Federal Reserve Bulletin*.

The figures are available on the third Friday after the week containing the 12th of the month, which falls on the first or second Friday of the month following the month to which they refer. On the day the monthly numbers are released, the Commissioner of Labor Statistics reports on recent unemployment and employment trends to the Joint Economic Committee of Congress. The monthly data are revised every January for the previous five years based on updated monthly seasonal factors.

Content

Unemployment figures measure the number of persons 16 years and older who do not have jobs and are available for and actively seeking work. The labor force is defined as the sum of employed and unemployed persons living in the United States. Both citizens and foreigners are included. The unemployment rate is the percentage of persons in the labor force who are unemployed and is calculated by the following formula:

$$\text{Unemployment rate} = \frac{\text{Unemployed persons}}{\text{Employed + unemployed persons (labor force)}} \times 100$$

EMPLOYED PERSONS are defined as nonfarm and farm workers 16 years and older who are not institutionalized. The definition includes full-time and part-time employees at paid jobs who work at least one hour a week, self-employed workers, and unpaid workers in family businesses who work at least 15 hours a week. Because the employment measures count persons rather than jobs, individuals holding two or more jobs are counted only once—in the job they work the most hours during a week. Persons who are temporarily not working because of illness, vacation, strike, or lockout are included as employed whether or not they are paid while absent from work. (These definitions differ from an alternative measure discussed in *employment*; contrasts in the two measures are analyzed in that section.)

UNEMPLOYED PERSONS are defined as those who have sought a job at least once in the previous four weeks through such actions as applying for work with an employer, answering a newspaper advertisement, visiting an employment agency, or checking with a friend or relative. They include individuals who collect unemployment insurance as well as those who are not eligible for unemployment insurance (for example, formerly employed workers who have exhausted their unemployment insurance or former students who have not accumulated job-related unemployment benefits). Students are counted as unemployed if they sought work and are available at least for part-time jobs.

DISCOURAGED WORKERS are not counted as unemployed. These are workers who say they want a job, but are not seeking work because they feel there are no jobs available in the local labor market or believe they don't qualify for the existing job vacancies.

There are two official national unemployment rates. One covers civilian workers and the resident armed forces (stationed in the U.S.), while the other covers only civilian workers. Unemployment rates are also calculated for large states and metropolitan areas and by demographic components of workers such as age, race, sex, and marital status of adults in the household.

Table 42 shows the two official unemployment rate figures and six supplementary analytic measures. The official figures, referred to as U–5a and U–5b, differ only in that one covers the total of civilian workers and the U.S. armed forces stationed in the United States, while the other covers only civilian workers. The unemployment rate for the total is typically 0.1 percentage point lower than the civilian rate. The six supplementary measures calculate rates based on duration of unemployment, reason for unemployment, age of the unemployed, and full-time or part-time work status; rates including discouraged workers are also provided. These measures provide a range of unemployment rates significantly below and above the official rates.

The unemployment figures are seasonally adjusted.

Methodology

Unemployment figures are obtained from a survey of a sample of households conducted for the Bureau of Labor Statistics by the

Table 42

Alternative Unemployment Rates Using Varying Definitions of Unemployment and the Labor Force (percent)

	1987:4Q[a]
U–1	Persons unemployed 15 weeks or longer as a percent of the civilian labor force	1.5
U–2	Job losers as a percent of the civilian labor force[b]	2.7
U–3	Unemployed persons 25 years and over as a percent of the civilian labor force	4.5
U–4	Unemployed full-time jobseekers as a percent of the full-time civilian labor force	5.5
U–5a*	**Total unemployed (16 years and older) as a percent of the labor force, including the resident armed forces**	**5.8**
U–5b*	**Total unemployment (16 years and older) as a percent of the civilian labor force**	**5.9**
U–6	Total full-time jobseekers plus 1/2 part-time jobseekers plus 1/2 total on part-time for economic reasons as a percent of the civilian labor force less 1/2 of the part-time labor force[c]	8.1
U–7	U–6 plus discouraged workers as a percent of the civilian labor force plus discouraged workers less 1/2 of the part-time labor force	8.8

*Official unemployment rates.

[a]Fourth quarter of 1987.

[b]Job losers are unemployed because they were laid off or fired.

[c]Part-time for economic reasons refers to persons who wish to work full-time but who are working less than 35 hours a week because of slack work, materials shortages, or other factors beyond their control.

Census Bureau. In 1987, of 91.5 million total American households, the survey sample included approximately 60,000 households. Census interviewers visit or telephone households during the calendar week that includes the 19th day of the month and ask respondents about their labor force activity during the week that includes the 12th day of the month.

The sample is representative of the distribution of households in small and large metropolitan and rural areas. It undergoes a major revision every ten years to reflect the decennial population census. The figures also are updated annually on a limited basis to reflect current changes in residential locations due to new construction. *Housing starts* data are used to make these revisions. Four to five percent of the sample households are not interviewed because the residents are not found at home after repeated calls or they refuse to participate in the survey.

In order to reduce the reporting burden on any group of households, the sample is divided into eight subsamples (panels) that are rotated over a 16-month period. Each subsample is surveyed for 4 consecutive months, is then dropped from the survey for 8 months, and subsequently resurveyed for the 4 following months. At the end of the 16 months, the subsample is eliminated from the sample and is replaced with a new panel of households. The result of this procedure is that every month 25 percent of households in the sample are either new to the survey or are returning to it after an 8-month hiatus; correspondingly, 25 percent of the sample households drop out of the survey every month.

Accuracy

In two of three cases, a monthly change in the unemployment rate of at least plus or minus 0.2 percentage point is regarded as statistically significant. Although a change of zero or plus or minus 0.1 percentage point is not statistically significant for one month, cumulative changes of 0.1 percentage point in the same direction for two or more consecutive months are statistically significant. If the confidence standard is raised to 19 of 20 cases, only monthly changes of plus or minus 0.3 percentage point are significant.

Relevance

The unemployment rate is a major indicator of the degree to which the economy provides jobs for those seeking work. It is a key consideration when the President, Congress, and Federal Reserve Board determine whether economic growth should be stimulated or restrained (see Relevance under *gross national product*). In general, there is an inverse relationship between unemployment and the *gross national product* which is referred to as Okun's Law. In the late 1980s, this relationship functioned roughly as follows: the yearly unemployment rate remains the same if annual real GNP increases by 2.5 percent, with every 1 percentage point growth in real GNP above 2.5 percent lowering the unemployment rate by 0.5 percentage point, and every 1 percentage point growth in real GNP below 2.5 percent raising unemployment by 0.5 percentage point. These figures reflect the relationship that averages out over the years but does not hold in every year.

The unemployment rate is also used to analyze trade-offs between unemployment and inflation. In an adaptation of the concept referred to as the Phillips Curve, the unemployment rate is contrasted with the *consumer price index* in an attempt to find a balance between lower unemployment and higher inflation. This kind of analysis is used to assess goals for minimum unemployment and inflation rates such as are included in the Full Employment and Balanced Growth Act of 1978 (Humphrey-Hawkins Act).

In addition, the unemployment rate determines when federally financed supplementary unemployment benefits go into effect for particular localities when unemployment is persistently high. These benefits supplement regular state-provided unemployment benefits which have been exhausted and are triggered by a formula that includes both the national unemployment rate and state or metropolitan area unemployment rates.

Recent Trends

The unemployment rate showed a fluctuating pattern over the 1975–87 period. For all workers, unemployment declined in the late 1970s to a low of 5.8 percent in 1979, then rose to 9.5 percent in 1982 and 1983, and subsequently declined to 6.1 percent in 1987.

Table 43

Official Unemployment Rates
(percent)

	All workers: civilian and armed forces	Civilian workers
1975	8.3%	8.5%
1976	7.6	7.7
1977	6.9	7.1
1978	6.0	6.1
1979	5.8	5.8
1980	7.0	7.1
1981	7.5	7.6
1982	9.5	9.7
1983	9.5	9.6
1984	7.4	7.5
1985	7.1	7.2
1986	6.9	7.0
1987	6.1	6.2

References from Primary Data Source

Bureau of Labor Statistics, U.S. Department of Labor, *BLS Handbook of Methods*, April 1988, Chapter 1.

Bureau of Labor Statistics, U.S. Department of Labor, *How the Government Measures Unemployment*, Report 742, September 1987.

John E. Bregger, "The Current Population Survey: A Historical Perspective and BLS' Role," *Monthly Labor Review*, June 1984.

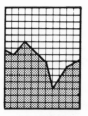

UNIT LABOR COSTS

Unit labor costs (ULC) represent the relationship of labor costs per hour to *productivity*. When employee compensation per hour increases more (or declines less) than productivity, ULC increase. Similarly, when compensation increases less (or declines more) than productivity, ULC decline. ULC also may be considered as compensation per unit of output, or the share that compensation is of output.

Where and When Available

The measure of unit labor costs (ULC) is provided on a quarterly basis by the Bureau of Labor Statistics in the U.S. Department of Labor. The data are published in a monthly press release and in two BLS monthly magazines, the *Monthly Labor Review* and *Employment and Earnings*. Secondary sources include *Economic Indicators* and *Business Conditions Digest*.

Preliminary figures for the immediately preceding quarter are provided in the second month following the quarter (May for the first quarter, August for the second quarter, November for the third quarter, and February for the fourth quarter). The data are available at the same time as the *productivity* figures and follow soon after publication of the *gross national product* measures. The data are initially revised in the subsequent two months. Additional revisions are made annually every September, and still

231

more comprehensive benchmark revisions are made about every six years.

Content

ULC are defined as the ratio of compensation per hour to *productivity*. This is equivalent to the ratio of compensation to output, because the per hour terms in the numerator and denominator cancel out algebraically as shown in the following formula:

$$\text{ULC} = \frac{\dfrac{\text{Compensation*}}{\text{Labor hours*}}}{\text{Productivity}} = \frac{\dfrac{\text{Compensation*}}{\text{Labor hours}\dagger}}{\dfrac{\text{Real GNP}\ddagger}{\text{Labor hours}\dagger}} = \frac{\text{Compensation}}{\text{Real GNP}} = \text{Compensation per unit of output}$$

*Wages and fringe benefits and the wage component of self-employment income.
†Paid employees, the self-employed, and unpaid family workers.
‡Business sector or nonfarm business sector.

The employee compensation component of ULC covers wages and salaries, fringe benefits, and the wage element of income from self-employment (it excludes the profit component of self-employment). ULC are provided as an index.

Separate figures are developed for the business sector, the nonfarm business sector, and the total of all manufacturing industries. They are based on real *gross national product* data adjusted to eliminate those components of the GNP that would cause an inappropriate measure of productivity because (a) the output indicator used is also an input measure or (b) the output and input data are inconsistent. The business sector includes for-profit enterprise and government enterprise; it excludes not-for-profit organizations, general government (general government is financed mainly by taxes while government enterprises are financed mainly by user fees), household employment, owner-occupied housing, and profit flows of American companies abroad into the

United States. The nonfarm business sector figures also exclude farming.

The ULC indexes are currently based on 1977 = 100.

The ULC figures are seasonally adjusted.

Methodology

The compensation data are obtained from the income side of the *gross national product* which in turn are based on *employment* payroll and household surveys, *average weekly hours*, and average hourly earnings. An additional estimate is made for the wage component of self-employment income based on data on hours worked by proprietors from the household survey of *employment*; the estimate assumes that proprietors work for the same hourly earnings as employees in the industry. Productivity is based on figures for *gross national product*, *employment*, and *average weekly hours* as described in *productivity*.

Accuracy

There are no estimates of sampling or revision error for the ULC figures.

Relevance

ULC figures indicate inflationary cost pressures. When ULC rise significantly, businesses may raise prices to maintain profit margins. Analogously, when ULC rise slightly or decline, profit margins can be maintained with little or no price increases or even price declines. There is a two-way street between ULC and prices, however, because ULC are affected by cost of living wage increases made to compensate for inflation. Moreover, in addition to ULC, prices reflect demand for goods and services, production costs other than ULC such as purchased materials prices, interest rates, the impact of weather on food, and the effect on energy prices of actions taken by the Organization of Petroleum

Table 44

Unit Labor Costs
(annual percent change)

	Business sector	Nonfarm business sector	Manufacturing
1975	7.6%	7.8%	9.1%
1976	5.9	5.7	3.5
1977	6.0	6.1	5.4
1978	7.6	7.7	6.6
1979	11.1	11.2	9.7
1980	10.9	11.0	11.7
1981	7.7	8.3	7.3
1982	8.3	8.4	6.2
1983	1.4	1.0	−2.5
1984	1.5	1.8	−1.9
1985	2.4	2.8	0.3
1986	2.1	2.2	0.5
1987	3.1	3.1	−1.2

Exporting Countries to control oil production. Thus, ULC are an important, but not necessarily determining, factor of price movements and *inflation*. As in the case of *productivity*, quarterly changes in ULC reflect short-term movements in output associated with changes in economic activity over the business cycle, and consequently ULC movements over several quarters should be observed to determine more basic trends.

Recent Trends

Increases in ULC in the business and nonfarm business sectors rose during the late 1970s to a high of 11 percent in 1979 and 1980. The rate of increase then slowed to under 2 percent in 1983 and 1984, and subsequently began rising again to 3 percent in 1987.

ULC in manufacturing rose in the late 1970s to nearly a 12

percent increase in 1980. The rate of increase slowed to 6 percent in 1982 and subsequently declined in three of the five years during 1983–87, with increases of only 0.3 and 0.5 percent in the other two years.

Reference from Primary Data Source

Bureau of Labor Statistics, U.S. Department of Labor, *BLS Handbook of Methods*, April 1988, Chapter 10.

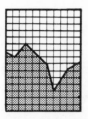

VALUE OF THE DOLLAR

The value of the dollar represents the foreign exchange price of the U.S. dollar in relation to other nations' currencies. If the dollar rises in value (and offsetting changes in the prices of exported and imported goods and services are not made), U.S. exports become more expensive to foreigners and imports become less expensive to Americans. If the dollar falls in value (and offsetting changes in the prices of exported and imported goods and services are not made), U.S. exports become less expensive to foreigners and imports become more expensive to Americans. Various measures of the value of the dollar show different movements because they include different countries and are based on different concepts and methodologies. The data are provided in nominal values (market exchange rates) and in real values (purchasing power corrected for inflation).

Where and When Available

Monthly indexes of the value of the dollar are provided by the Federal Reserve Board, International Monetary Fund, Morgan Guaranty Trust Company of New York, and Federal Reserve Bank of Dallas. The FRB index is published in a press release and in the monthly *Federal Reserve Bulletin*; the IMF index is published in the monthly *International Financial Statistics*; the Morgan index is published in *Weekly International Economic Data* and in the bimonthly *World Financial Markets*; and the FR Dallas index is published in a monthly statistical release.

The FRB figures are available weekly, for the previous week, and monthly, two days after the month to which they refer. The Morgan index is available daily. The IMF and FR Dallas figures are available 30 days after the month to which they refer. Measures of the real value of the dollar are published along with the nominal figures by Morgan and the FR Dallas; real values for the FRB index are available annually in the *Economic Report of the President*.

The Federal Reserve Board, IMF, and Morgan indexes are not routinely revised, except for the Morgan real effective exchange rate which is revised weekly. The FR Dallas indexes are revised for the previous five months, and the index weights are revised every year.

Content

The value of the dollar represents the combined average foreign exchange price of the currencies of a group of nations in relation to the U.S. dollar. In contrast to the nominal values which focus on the exchange value of the currencies, the real values measure the rate of exchange in terms of the constant-dollar cost of U.S. exports and imports adjusted for *inflation* at home and abroad. All of the indexes represent only nations with market economies (socialist nations are not represented in the indexes). The FRB, Morgan, and IMF indexes include 10, 15, and 17 industrial nations, respectively, and the FR Dallas index includes all of the 131 industrial and industrializing nations that trade with the United States (Table 45). Industrial nations have production technologies similar to those in the United States, while industrializing nations have less advanced technologies. The main difference among the indexes is the much more comprehensive coverage of the FR Dallas index. (Additional indexes developed by Morgan include some industrializing nations.)

The real value of the dollar measures are provided for the

Federal Reserve Board, Morgan, and FR Dallas indexes, but not for the IMF index. The base periods of the value of the dollar indexes currently are: Federal Reserve Board (March 1973 = 100); Morgan Guaranty (1980–82 = 100); International Monetary Fund (1980 = 100); and FR Dallas (1973: first quarter = 100).

The value of the dollar indexes are not seasonally adjusted.

Methodology

The four value-of-the-dollar indexes all use geometric averaging to calculate the percent change in each nation's currency between the base period and the current period. Geometric averaging (as opposed to arithmetic averaging) insures that currencies having large changes in foreign exchange values do not influence the index more than currencies having small changes. (Technically, geometric averaging is done by taking the nth root of n numbers, and arithmetic averaging is the sum of n numbers divided by n.)

The indexes differ in the weights used to combine the foreign currencies into an index (see Index Numbers in the Introduction). In the definition of weights, "global" trade refers to a nation's trade with all other nations, and "bilateral" trade refers to a nation's trade with one other nation. There are also differences in the price indexes used to estimate the real value of the dollar.

The FRB weights are each nation's global export and import trade in manufactured, mineral, and agricultural goods in the 1972–76 period, valued in dollars. The real value of the dollar is based on differential movements in the *consumer price index* in the United States and other nations.

The MORGAN weights are bilateral export and import trade between the United States and other nations for manufactured goods in 1980, valued in dollars. The real value of the dollar is based on differential price movements of *producer price indexes* for intermediate and finished manufactured goods (except food and fuel) in the United States and other nations.

The IMF weights are each nation's global export and import

Table 45

National Coverage of Dollar Indexes

Federal Reserve Board	Morgan Guaranty Trust Co. of New York	International Monetary Fund	Federal Reserve Bank of Dallas
(10 nations)	(15 nations)	(17 nations)	(131 nations. All U.S. trading partners with market economies.)
—	Australia	Australia	
—	Austria	Austria	
Belgium	Belgium	Belgium	
Canada	Canada	Canada	
—	Denmark	Denmark	
—	—	Finland	
France	France	France	
Germany	Germany	Germany	
—	—	Ireland	
Italy	Italy	Italy	
Japan	Japan	Japan	
Netherlands	Netherlands	Netherlands	
—	Norway	Norway	
—	Spain	Spain	
Sweden	Sweden	Sweden	
Switzerland	Switzerland	Switzerland	
United Kingdom	United Kingdom	United Kingdom	

trade in manufactured, mineral, and agricultural goods in 1977, valued in dollars. The weights are derived from the IMF's multilateral exchange rate model (MERM) of 18 industrial nations. The MERM includes the effects of the following on each nation's *balance of trade*: the size of trade flows, price elasticities in the relationship between foreign exchange values and the volume of trade, and the feedback of exchange rate changes on domestic costs and prices. The result is that the MERM weights reflect the contribution of a unilateral change in each nation's currency to the total change in the trade balance.

The FR DALLAS weights are the bilateral export and import

trade between the United States and each nation in manufactured, mineral, and agricultural goods on a current basis, valued in dollars. The weights are changed every year based on moving averages of the trade in the most recent three years, in contrast to the other indexes, where weights are fixed for a single period. The real value of the dollar is based on differential movements of the *consumer price index* in the United States and other nations.

Accuracy

There are no estimates of sampling or revision error for the value-of-the-dollar indexes.

Relevance

The value of the dollar affects the American economy through several avenues. It determines the competitive position of American goods in export markets and domestically, and also affects inflation and Federal Reserve Board monetary policies.

A "low dollar" tends to boost production and inflation at home while a "high" dollar tends to lower production and inflation, although changes in the dollar are not transmitted to prices in a one-to-one relationship. Part or all of the dollar changes may be offset by opposing changes in export and import prices as American and foreign exporters try to maintain market shares and profit margins. Thus, a fall in the dollar may be followed by some increase in American export prices and in import prices, while a rise in the dollar may be followed by some decrease in export prices and in import prices. These "pass throughs" of price changes that partly or fully offset changes in the value of the dollar can be calculated as noted in *import and export price indexes*.

The value of the dollar also affects the monetary policies by which the Federal Reserve Board manages the economy. For example, the large deficits in the *balance of trade* in the 1980s were financed, in part, by foreigners who invested funds in the United States. If the dollar declines or is expected to decline in the future, this funding may be cut back. In this situation, the Federal Reserve is faced with the dilemma of accelerating growth in the *money supply*, which may heat up *inflation*, or allowing a slower growth in the money supply, which may raise *interest rates* and bring on a recession. For the Federal Reserve Board, this international dimension complicates the development of appropriate policies for the domestic economy.

Recent Trends

Over the 1975–87 period, the FRB, Morgan, and IMF indexes generally moved in similar patterns, although with some distinctions, while the FR Dallas index moved much differently (in nominal values). The FRB, Morgan, and IMF indexes typically declined while the FR Dallas index rose during 1975–80; the

Table 46

**Value-of-the-Dollar Indexes: Nominal Values
(annual percent change)**

	Federal Reserve Board	Morgan Guaranty Trust Co. of New York	International Monetary Fund	Federal Reserve Bank of Dallas
1975	−2.9	0.1	−1.0	2.4
1976	7.2	3.6	5.2	4.4
1977	−2.2	−0.4	−0.5	2.4
1978	−10.6	−8.2	−8.6	−2.0
1979	−4.7	−1.5	−2.1	1.1
1980	−0.8	−0.1	0.2	3.0
1981	17.7	9.7	12.7	11.5
1982	13.3	10.4	11.7	15.2
1983	7.5	4.0	5.8	12.6
1984	10.4	7.1	7.9	14.2
1985	3.5	3.8	4.5	12.6
1986	−21.6	−16.5	−18.4	−2.3
1987	−13.6	−11.2	−11.8	−1.6
1975–80	−11.3	−6.8	−6.1	9.0
1980–85	63.8	40.0	50.2	86.0
1985–87	−32.3	−25.9	−28.0	−3.9
1975–87	−1.6	−3.3	1.4	95.9

FRB, Morgan, and IMF indexes rose much less than the FR Dallas index during 1980–85; and the FRB, Morgan, and IMF indexes declined much more than the FR Dallas index during 1985–87. The result for the entire 12-year period is that, in 1987, the FRB and Morgan indexes are slightly below 1975 levels, the IMF index is slightly above 1975, and the FR Dallas index is considerably above 1975.

The differential patterns of the FR Dallas index reflect the effect of including industrializing nations in the FR Dallas index. This can be significant for analyzing prospects for the *balance of trade* because of the importance of industrializing nations in our foreign trade.

There are noticeable differences in the year-to-year movements among the FRB, Morgan, and IMF indexes. Generally, the FRB index shows the largest short-term changes and the Morgan index the smallest, with the IMF index midway but closer to the Morgan index.

References from Primary Data Sources

B. Dianne Pauls, "Measuring the Foreign-Exchange Value of the Dollar," *Federal Reserve Bulletin*, June 1987.

Federal Reserve Board, "Index of the Weighted-Average Exchange Value of the U.S. Dollar: Revision," *Federal Reserve Bulletin*, August 1978.

Morgan Guaranty Trust Company of New York, "Dollar index confusion," *World Financial Markets*, October/November 1986.

International Monetary Fund, "Introduction," *International Financial Statistics*, monthly; and Jacques R. Artus and Anne Kenny McGuirk, "A Revised Version of the Multilateral Exchange Rate Model," *Staff Papers*, June 1981.

W. Michael Cox, "A Comprehensive New Real Dollar Exchange Rate Index," *Economic Review* (Federal Reserve Bank of Dallas), March 1987.

W. Michael Cox, "A New Alternative Trade-Weighted Dollar Exchange Rate Index," *Economic Review* (Federal Reserve Bank of Dallas), September 1986.